Fun English 1

Teacher's Guide

Longman

Jill Leighton and Laura Sánchez Donovan

with **Izabella Hearn**

Pearson Education
Edinburgh Gate
Harlow, Essex CM20 2JE
England
and Associated Companies throughout the World

www.longman.com

First published by Pearson Educación 2001
Original edition © Pearson Educación and Jill Leighton and Laura Sánchez
Donovan 2001
This edition © Pearson Education Limited 2003
Fifth impression 2010

Printed in Malaysia, KHL

ISBN: 978-0-582-78942-5

Illustrations: Fernando Puertollano, Duñaiturria+Vidal, I.C. Claroscuro, S.L.,
Aurora Losada

Design: Marta Illescas Núñez (Coordinator), Alfredo Casaccia, Soledad
San Segundo

This edition produced for the publishers by Bluestone Press, Charlbury

CONTENTS

Components

This introduction will help you find your way around **Fun English 1** before beginning the course.

Fun English makes use of a wealth of materials and a wide range of educational strategies appropriate for young learners, taking the children as the starting point: their learning styles, the way they interact with each other, and their interests and needs. Learning should always be a meaningful and, as the title suggests, fun experience. *Fun English* aims to involve, motivate and amuse the children, while creating an enjoyable teaching and learning experience for both you and your pupils. We hope you enjoy teaching with *Fun English!*

PUPIL'S BOOK
with stickers

The *Pupil's Book* consists of eight presentation units. At the end of each unit there is a *My English dictionary* page which represents the key language of the unit and a set of cutout cards for the children to prepare and 'play' with. There are three festivals lessons at the end of the book which can be incorporated into the teaching programme as the event arises. They include *Happy Birthday, Christmas,* and *Easter.* The stickers are to be used with listening activities in the *Pupil's Book.* While children thoroughly enjoy manipulating stickers, they also help develop hand-eye coordination and perception skills.

WORKBOOK

The *Workbook* maintains the same structure as the *Pupil's Book,* and provides reinforcement and consolidation of the language developed in the core lessons. The activities build on a variety of learning strategies and techniques that the children are familiar with in other areas of their learning, such as comparing, drawing, classifying, matching, observing, colouring, and ordering.

TEACHER'S GUIDE

The *Teacher's Guide* includes lesson by lesson teaching notes. The teaching notes take a three step approach to each lesson, and include suggestions for reinforcement and extension at the end. The teaching programme can be found at the beginning of the guide, and a *Resource Bank* of photocopiable material and Evaluation material at the end.

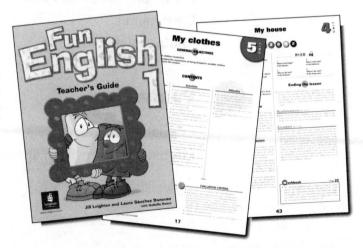

4

AUDIO CD AND CASSETTE

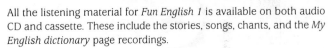

All the listening material for *Fun English 1* is available on both audio CD and cassette. These include the stories, songs, chants, and the *My English dictionary* page recordings.

FLASHCARDS

A pack of 64 illustrated *flashcards* represent key language from *Fun English 1* and *2*. Suggestions for using the *flashcards* are integrated into the lesson procedures in the *Teacher's Guide*.

POSTERS

There are six posters to complement *Fun English 1* and *2*. Four of the posters represent topics related directly to the units, and two serve to develop the festivals of *Halloween* and *Christmas*.

Characteristics

OBJECTIVES OF FUN ENGLISH

When teaching English to children it is important to remember that while there are clear linguistic objectives, the learning process itself plays an important role in the children's development. **FUN ENGLISH** aims to attend to and foster this development. The key objectives are:

- To promote the wider educational experience through activities which develop those skills promoted in other learning areas, besides language skills.
- To develop the children's creativity and capture their imagination while learning English.
- To take a communicative approach to teaching the new language and lay down the foundations to develop oral comprehension and production.
- To make the social and moral issues dealt with an integral part of the learning experience.
- To foster confidence and enjoyment when communicating in English by promoting a stress-free and play-like atmosphere, and to provide the children with the maximum opportunity for success.

THE TEACHING SYLLABUS

- Most children starting with *Fun English 1* will have had no previous contact with the English language, so the syllabus takes as its starting point the children themselves in order to make the learning meaningful. The language syllabus stems from specific topics which are relevant to the children's own experiences, and from concepts that the children are already familiar with in their mother tongue. In level 2 of *Fun English* this language is consolidated and extended.

- The social and moral issues integrated into the units of *Fun English* have been carefully chosen to reflect issues relevant to the children's lives. They are often presented in the stories and the children are encouraged to reflect on the issues in the lesson.

- Within any one class of children there are differences in learning styles and levels. The variety of activity types and the reinforcement and extension activities are designed to attend to these differences. At the same time, any established syllabus should always be adapted to the particular children concerned.

METHODOLOGICAL APPROACH

- Children learn by the things that they see, hear and do. If the teaching goal is to carry out the activity rather than concentrating on the language itself, very often the children become immersed in the activity and the learning takes care of itself. For this reason the activities in *Fun English* involve the children in tasks, games, songs and stories where the language itself is not the overall objective.

- The course aims to actively involve the children in the lessons. In the *Hello* lessons at the beginning of the course the children make personalised puppets which they work with throughout the year, directly identifying themselves with the characters Banana and Chocolate, and the topics developed.

- As has been mentioned, in any one class different learning styles and levels exist. Research shows that some learners are more right-brained, while others are more left-brained. To maximise learning, both hemispheres of the brain need to be used, and this is reflected in the learning techniques chosen in *Fun English*. Some of the techniques implemented for more right-brained learners are: movement, arts and crafts, guessing work, looking for links and connections, and activities which involve the emotions. For left-brained learners some of the activity types involve sequencing, learning songs, and producing language.

- Much of the new language is presented and practised through TPR (Total Physical Response). The focus on instructions and response in TPR provides a cooperative and fun atmosphere where children feel at ease and are willing to join in. The situations and activities in the lessons invite them to demonstrate their comprehension of the new language whether they speak or not. The movement involved in TPR stimulates long term retention, helping to ensure a higher degree of success for the whole class.

EDUCATIONAL STRATEGIES

1. Banana and Chocolate, the class mascots

Banana and Chocolate are two affectionate characters that the children can recognise and identify with immediately. They bring the class to life through their stories and adventures, allow the teacher to create an important communicative context for the children, and they make the class FUN. Using the *flashcards*, Banana and Chocolate can speak to the children, and the children can speak back. This promotes an atmosphere of trust and security in the classroom. Socialisation is an important element in the development of children at this age, and the interactions between Banana, Chocolate and the children, the children with each other, and the children with the teacher, all help contribute to this socialisation process as well as creating a communicative context in which to situate the new language.

Characteristics

2. Stories

Children enjoy and learn from stories from a very early age. In *Fun English 1*, original stories based on the adventures of Banana and Chocolate are included in each unit. They serve to practise and consolidate the key language, and to situate the vocabulary in a new context. The language of the stories has been carefully structured and graded to help comprehension, but without distracting from the meaning or humour. The stories are self-contained and highly visual, aiming for maximum comprehension on the part of the children. The support of the recorded material with different voices and sound effects is an invaluable aid for the children to experience real language in context.

The stories have been specially written so as to be conceptually and cognitively appropriate as well as enjoyable. They provide an excellent means to linking English with the work the children are doing in other areas, and many of the stories have an underlying message which the teacher can develop further in the classroom.

The children can be actively involved in the storytelling through answering questions, and prediction and repetition work. The *Teacher's Guide* provides a wealth of ideas to exploit the language learning opportunities that the stories offer, plus suggestions for acting out the stories.

3. Songs and chants

Songs and chants have been included in each unit of *Fun English 1*. Most of the songs have been written specifically for the course, others are traditional songs which have been adapted to the context and language of the syllabus. The songs and chants provide the children with oral skills practice, they provide models for intonation and stress patterns in the language, and help the children to assimilate the language in a motivating way. They also lend themselves to mime and actions, for which guidelines are laid out in the *Teacher's Guide*.

4. Arts and crafts

Art and craft activities are included in most of the units. They are suggested either in the main lesson procedure, or in the sections for reinforcement and extension. These activities have been realistically designed, requiring little preparation on the part of the teacher and needing only simple materials to be carried out. It is strongly recommended to include some form of art / craft activity on a regular basis to help the children become skilful with their hands. Further,

it is important for the children to have work which can be displayed, and that they can feel proud of. Many children are strongly kinaesthetic and learn best by 'doing'. Craft projects are an excellent way to give them a chance to succeed and progress. The photocopiable pages in the *Resource Bank* will help to make these activities as practical and rewarding as possible.

5. Games

A number of games are included in the *Pupil's Book* and further suggestions for games can be found in the teaching notes and in the *My English dictionary* and *Card games* sections of the *Resource Bank*. Children play games as part of their everyday experience, and their value can very often exceed that of practising a specific language element. Through games, children learn to interact and co-operate with their friends, and since the emphasis is on participation and enjoyment, games create an opportunity for natural language in a familiar situation. The games in *Fun English* are not intended to be highly competitive but rather to immerse the children in the 'playing'.

SKILLS WORK

- The listening skill takes priority in level 1 of *Fun English*. The children are presented with the language through a variety of educational strategies, and oral production takes place once the children have been able to assimilate the language. This takes time! The language is constantly recycled throughout level 1 and again consolidated in level 2, through a variety of situations and contexts. Children need this period of language input before they are expected to produce the language.

- The activities in lesson four of each unit in the *Pupil's Book* develop pre-writing skills, hand-eye coordination and fine motor control. In level 2 the children start to read in English (individual word recognition) and can start to form the shapes of the letters and words on paper by tracing or copying if you wish.

Organisational structure of Fun English

- **FUN ENGLISH 1** contains eight key presentation units, plus three extra festivals lessons. The units are made up of six lessons and each includes a *My English dictionary* page and a set of cutout vocabulary cards. The organisational development of a unit is laid out below, lesson by lesson. The festivals lessons, *Birthday*, *Christmas* and *Easter*, provide extra material to be used as the festivals arise in the year. The *Birthday* lesson can be used when one or several children in the class celebrate their birthday.

- The **Workbook** provides consolidation for the key language presented in the *Pupil's Book*. Although the *Workbook* is an additional component, the pages are directly related to those of the *Pupil's Book*. A variety of learning strategies and techniques that the children are familiar with - drawing, classifying, matching, observing, colouring, relating, etc. - are used.

- The **Teacher's Guide** contains many teaching ideas and suggestions. The teaching notes for the units are organised lesson by lesson, and each lesson is divided into three basic steps: *Beginning the lesson* generally provides an opportunity to 'warm up' the class with revision of language through a game, song or chant. *Developing the lesson* presents and practises the main language points of the current lesson, and *Ending the lesson* 'winds down' the class in a more game-like and fun way. Additional suggestions for reinforcement and extension are included at the end of each lesson.

LESSON 1

Banana and Chocolate present the new topic and key vocabulary for the unit in the first lesson of the **Pupil's Book** through a chant, song or listening activity. The icons on the page clearly indicate the activity types to be carried out.

The **Workbook** practises some element of the new language through educational strategies suitable for children of this age group. In this lesson an activity designed to promote perception and interpretation skills is used. The characters bring humour to the learning situation.

LESSON 2

- Every second and third page of a **Pupil's Book** unit includes a double page illustration to provide a context for the new language. In this lesson children identify key vocabulary in the illustration, helped by the columns on either side. Again the characters bring a fun element to the lesson, playing a central role in presenting and practising the language.
Language is constantly recycled throughout the course. Here, the family vocabulary from unit 3 is consolidated in a new context.

- The **Workbook** provides more practice for the new language. In this activity the children are invited to bring skills they are developing in the maths class into the English lesson.

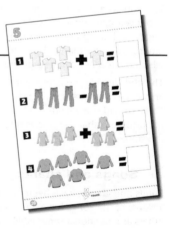

LESSON 3

The third lesson of the **Pupil's Book** again works with the double page illustration, this time developing the situation and language in greater detail through a listening activity.

The **Workbook** activities include fun, puzzle-like tasks, but always with the aim of consolidating the key language.

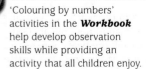

LESSON 4

Lesson four of the **Pupil's Book** is designed to develop the finer motor skills and hand-eye coordination. This is done through pre-writing activities, or using stickers. In this lesson the children dress Banana and Chocolate in their carnival costumes.

'Colouring by numbers' activities in the **Workbook** help develop observation skills while providing an activity that all children enjoy.

LESSON 5

The stories in the **Pupil's Book** are developed in lesson 5. They consolidate the language, provide humour through the characters Banana and Chocolate and present social and moral issues. The lesson notes in the *Teacher's Guide* provide suggestions for role plays once the children are familiar with the story.

More consolidation of key vocabulary is provided in the **Workbook**.

LESSON 6

All the key language from the unit is represented visually in the **My English dictionary** page. The *Teacher's Guide* includes suggestions for pronunciation work and games to be played around the dictionary page. The *Yaka Boo!* section encourages the children to reflect on the things they are learning and star stickers are used as awards on completing the unit.

In the **Workbook,** the children are invited to personalise the things they are learning through a drawing activity.

CUTOUT CARDS

The cutout cards come at the end of each unit, but can be used at different stages during the development of the unit. There are a variety of suggestions outlined in the teaching notes.

Evaluation

EVALUATION plays an integral part in the teaching / learning process. It can provide important information not only about the performance of the children but also about the types of materials used and the teaching methods undertaken. In *Fun English* evaluation works on the following levels:

- **Formative evaluation**
  Suggestions for formative evaluation are included in the teaching notes throughout the unit period. They involve the direct and systematic observation of the children's daily work in the classroom. A photocopiable evaluation chart to record this classroom observation can be found on page 92 of this guide.

- **Summative evaluation**
  Traditional tests sometimes give an inaccurate picture of children's abilities due to the stress and anxiety which they can feel. In *Fun English* the summative evaluation is carried out at the end of each unit with the *Revision Sheets*. There are *Revision Sheets* for each unit. They have been designed to reflect the fun, 'game-like' quality of the activity types undergone throughout the course and

are all listening activities to which the children respond. Instructions for carrying out each *Revision Sheet* are clearly explained at the beginning of the Evaluation section. To do the *Revision Sheets*, first hand out a copy to each child and go through the activities on the page. Then follow the instructions indicated.

The marking scheme appears on each sheet and a photocopiable record sheet for the results can be found on page 93 of this guide. Stars have been included on the *Revision Sheets* which the children can colour once they have been marked. In this way the children are invited to reflect on their performance.

- **Self-evaluation**
  At the end of every unit the *My English dictionary* page provides the opportunity to go over the key language with the children and assess their progress. This is accompanied by the *Yaka Boo!* chant and indicates the end of the unit. The children are invited by Banana and Chocolate to take one of their star stickers and to stick it on the page. Explain to the children that the unit has finished and congratulate them on what they have learnt about the particular topic in English.

Additional resources

• My English dictionary •
You will find a selection of activities on page 76 of this guide to use with the **My English dictionary** pages at the end of each unit in the *Pupil's Book*. They are designed to both recycle and consolidate the language the children have learnt in the unit, and to provide the opportunity for the children to start to work with and understand a language reference in a fun and motivating way.

The activities work with the key vocabulary of the course and include suggestions for the children to work either individually or to play games in pairs or teams. They can be easily adapted to work with the different word groups found on each of the picture dictionary pages.

• Card games •
The cutout cards in the *Pupil's Book* provide a valuable teaching resource for presenting,

practising and consolidating language. The preparation and use of the cards has been incorporated into the lesson notes, but you will also find a list of games to be played with the cards on page 77 of this guide. These games require active participation on the part of the children and take the emphasis off learning. They help create an atmosphere of play, very often the best way to foster the learning process.

Teaching programme

FUN ENGLISH

Hello!

GENERAL OBJECTIVES

- To learn the greetings *hello* and *goodbye*.
- To identify and name the main characters of the book.
- To introduce oneself in English.
- To develop a positive attitude towards English.

CONTENTS

Concepts

Functions
- To understand and use the greetings *hello* and *goodbye*.
- To learn the names of the main characters of the book.
- To say one's name using *I'm ...*
- To become familiar with some basic classroom language.
- To identify the sound /h/.

Linguistic exponents
- *Hello / Goodbye.* • *I'm ...* • *Open your books.* • *Colour.* • *Look.* • *Cut.* • *Fold.* • *Stick.* • *Point to.* • *Listen.* • *Sing.* • *What's your name? I'm ...*

Vocabulary
Banana, Chocolate, scissors, glue, puppets, present, book.

Activities

- Using non-linguistic aids (gestures, facial expressions ...) to help comprehension and elicit responses.
- Reciting and acting out chants to learn the new language.
- Making a personalised puppet.
- Pronouncing the sound /h/.

Attitudes

- Showing a positive attitude towards English.
- Participating willingly in classroom activities.
- Showing interest in doing the activities in a clean and tidy way.
- Treating classroom materials (scissors, glue, crayons ...) with care.
- Understanding the need to tidy up the classroom before the end of the lesson.

CROSS-CURRICULAR THEMES

- **Civic education:** Encouraging pupils to be polite by greeting each other in class (Lesson 1: *Developing the lesson;* Lesson 2: *Developing the lesson* and *Ending the lesson*).

EVALUATION CRITERIA

- Teacher's observation of attitude, effort and participation.
- Task analysis: Oral expression (Lesson 2: *Ending the lesson -* introducing oneself and greeting others). Class work (Lesson 2: *Developing the lesson -* making puppets).

My English class

GENERAL OBJECTIVES

- To talk about the classroom and classroom objects.
- To understand and respond to instructions related to classroom language.
- To create a friendly atmosphere in the classroom.

CONTENTS

Concepts

Functions
- To understand classroom instructions.
- To identify classroom objects.
- To count from one to four.
- To identify the colours: *green, red, blue, yellow* and *brown*.
- To learn how the colours are made.
- To understand the meaning of *happy / sad*.
- To learn the vocabulary from the picture dictionary.

Linguistic exponents
• Hello / Goodbye. • What's your name? I'm ...
• It's (green). • It's (a pencil). • This is (red).
• Thank you. • Yes / No. • Look! • Colour. • Point to. • Listen. • Sing. • Open / close your book.
• Find. • Mix. • Take. • Let's ... • Who's this?
• Stand up / sit down / jump. • Very good. • What colour? • Show me ... • What colour is (two)?
• What number is (red)? • (Blue) and (yellow) make (brown). • (Be) happy / sad. • (Chocolate) is happy / sad. (Chocolate) is / isn't (brown). • Banana's got a ... • I'm happy / sad.

Vocabulary
Teacher, pencil, book, rubber, crayon, scissors, glue, chair, green, red, blue, yellow, brown, yes, no, one, two, three, four, up, down, granny, star.

Activities

- Using non-linguistic aids (gestures, *flashcards*, objects ...) to help comprehension and elicit responses.
- Eliciting non-linguistic responses in the classroom.
- Reciting, singing and acting out chants and songs to learn the unit language.
- Using the answers *Yes / No.*
- Playing a guessing game to revise the classroom objects.
- Playing games to revise the colours.
- Playing games to revise the numbers.
- Listening to a story in English.
- Describing feelings with *happy / sad.*
- Playing an action game to follow instructions (*Chocolate Says ...*).
- Using the picture dictionary to consolidate the unit vocabulary.
- Completing the self-evaluation activity.
- Doing the evaluation activity at the end of the unit.

Attitudes

- Recognising the importance of helping others when they are in need.
- Participating willingly in class games and activities.
- Enjoying the songs, chants and games.
- Understanding the importance of keeping the classroom tidy and clean.
- Treating both the classroom materials (scissors, glue, crayons ...) and one's own material (book, cards ...) with care.
- Valuing one's work positively.

CROSS-CURRICULAR THEMES

- **Peace studies:** Encouraging pupils to get to know and help each other in the classroom in order to create a friendly atmosphere (Lesson 1: *Extension activity;* Lesson 2: *Extension activity;* Lesson 5: *Activity 2*).

EVALUATION CRITERIA

- Teacher's observation of attitude, effort and participation.
- Task Analysis: Oral expression (Lesson 1: *Beginning the lesson - introducing oneself*). Oral comprehension (Lesson 1: *Beginning the lesson* and Lesson 4: *Activity 1 - Following classroom instructions*).
- Answering questions for the teacher while doing the activities (Lesson 3: *Activity 2;* Lesson 4: *Ending the lesson – Colouring the numbers*).
- Doing the self-evaluation activity.
- Completing the *Revision Sheet for Unit 1* (*Teacher's Guide*, page 98).

2 UNIT

My body

GENERAL OBJECTIVES

- To identify and name the parts of the face and body.
- To enjoy learning about the celebration of Halloween.

CONTENTS

Concepts

Functions
- To identify the parts of the face and body.
- To learn about the celebration of Halloween.
- To learn vocabulary related to Halloween.
- To identify colours: *orange* and *black*.
- To identify the sound /s/.
- To understand the meaning of *big / small*.
- To learn vocabulary from the picture dictionary.

Linguistic exponents
• *Run.* • *Hold hands.* • *Hold up (the witch).* • *Touch (Chocolate's / your / your partner's nose).* • *Show me your (eyes).* • *(Green eyes) can go.* • *Who's this?* • *Yes / No.* • *Look and find.* • *How many (witches)?* • *What colour?* • *Up / down.* • *Let's ...* • *The monster's got ...* • *(Chocolate) is big / small.*

Vocabulary
Eyes, mouth, nose, arms, hands, legs, feet, black, orange, witch, monster, cat, ghost, pumpkin, skeleton, big, small.

Activities

- Using non-linguistic aids (gestures, *flashcards*, objects, posters ...) to help comprehension and elicit responses.
- Eliciting non-linguistic responses in the classroom.
- Reciting, singing and acting out chants and songs to learn the unit language.
- Using the answers *Yes / No.*
- Playing with puppets to revise the parts of the body.
- Making a skeleton.
- Doing a tracing activity to develop motor skills.
- Listening to a story in English to identify the meaning of *big* and *small.*
- Acting out the story.
- Playing action games to follow instructions.
- Using the Halloween poster to play a quiz.
- Playing a card game and using the picture dictionary to consolidate the unit vocabulary.
- Completing the self-evaluation activity.
- Doing the evaluation activity at the end of the unit.

Attitudes

- Enjoying the songs, chants and stories in English.
- Participating willingly in class games and activities.
- Recognising the importance of helping others when they are in difficulty.
- Showing interest in learning about a different culture.
- Keeping the classroom tidy and clean.

CROSS-CURRICULAR THEMES

- **Peace studies:** Valuing the importance and richness of cultural differences (Lesson 2: *Activity 1*; Lesson 3: *Reinforcement activity*).

EVALUATION CRITERIA

- Teacher's observation of attitude, effort and participation.
- Task Analysis: Oral comprehension (Lesson 2: *Activity 2* - Find and colour). Class work (Lesson 4: *Activity 2* - Skeleton cutout). Answering questions for the teacher while doing the activities (Lesson 2: *Activity 2* - Find and colour; *Ending the lesson* - Point to; Lesson 6: *Activity 1* - Show me).
- Doing the self-evaluation activity.
- Completing the *Revision Sheet for Unit 2* (*Teacher's Guide*, page 99).

My family

GENERAL OBJECTIVES

- To identify and learn the names of the members of the family.
- To recognise the importance of thinking about others.
- To talk about Christmas.

CONTENTS

Concepts

Functions

- To identify the members of the family.
- To learn about the celebration of Christmas.
- To learn vocabulary related to Christmas.
- To identify the numbers *five* and *six*.
- To revise vocabulary related to numbers, colours and the parts of the body.
- To understand a story in English.
- To understand the expressions: *Oh dear!* and *Happy Christmas!*
- To learn new vocabulary from the picture dictionary.

Linguistic exponents

• *Who's this?* • *This is my (mother).* • *What's this?* • *This is a (bell).* • *Smile.* • *Find (three) (mothers).* • *Show me (the mother).* • *Hold up (the sister).* • *How many (presents)?* • *Which is your favourite?* • *What number is this?* • *My (legs)!* • *Oh no!* • *Oh dear!* • *Happy Christmas!*

Vocabulary

Family, father, mother, brother, sister, baby, Father Christmas, snowman, star, presents, Christmas tree, bell, five, six, banana skin.

Activities

- Using non-linguistic aids (gestures, *flashcards,* objects, posters ...) to help comprehension and elicit responses.
- Eliciting non-linguistic responses in the classroom.
- Playing action games to revise vocabulary from previous units.
- Playing card games to consolidate the unit vocabulary.
- Reciting, singing and acting out the chants and songs to learn the unit language.
- Playing a game with the puppets to revise the names of the members of the family.
- Playing a guessing game and an ordering game while listening to a story in English.
- Making a Christmas card and a Christmas present.
- Using the *Happy Christmas poster* to revise the vocabulary and structures.
- Doing tracing and colouring activities to develop motor skills.
- Using the picture dictionary.
- Completing the self-evaluation activity.
- Doing the evaluation activity at the end of the unit.

Attitudes

- Recognising the importance of thinking about others, especially at Christmas.
- Recognising the importance of wearing the appropriate clothes according to the weather.
- Participating willingly in class games and activities.
- Enjoying the songs, chants and stories in English.

CROSS-CURRICULAR THEMES

- **Peace studies:** Recognising the importance of thinking and caring about others, especially at Christmas (Lesson 2: *Activity 1, Ending the lesson;* Lesson 3: *Activity 1*).
- **Health education:** Recognising the importance of being dressed in suitable clothes and shoes according to the weather (Lesson 5: *Developing the lesson*).

EVALUATION CRITERIA

- Teacher's observation of attitude, effort and participation.
- Task Analysis: Class work (Lesson 2: *Ending the lesson* - Making a Christmas card; Lesson 3: *Activity 1* - Making a Christmas present; *Activity 2* - Find and colour). Oral comprehension (Lesson 6: *Beginning the lesson* - Following instructions). Oral expression (Lesson 6: *Beginning the lesson* - Questions about the poster). Answering questions for the teacher while doing the activities (Lesson 2: *Ending the lesson;* Lesson 4: *Ending the lesson* - What number?; Lesson 6: *Beginning the lesson* - Questions about the poster).
- Doing the self-evaluation activity.
- Completing the *Revision Sheet for Unit 3 (Teacher's Guide,* page 100).

4 UNIT

My house

GENERAL OBJECTIVES

- To identify and name rooms in the house and items of furniture.
- To recognise the importance of helping out at home.

CONTENTS

Concepts

Functions

- To learn the word *house* and the names of the rooms in the house.
- To learn some furniture vocabulary and relate it to the corresponding rooms.
- To identify different household activities.
- To relate rooms and household activities through sounds.
- To revise vocabulary related to numbers, colours, parts of the body and members of the family.
- To learn about a traditional English children's game.
- To understand a story in English.
- To learn new vocabulary from the picture dictionary.

Linguistic exponents

• *Come with me.* • *Let's go to (Banana's house).* • *(My mother) is in the (living room.)* • *Point to the (living room).* • *Number (threes) go to the (bathroom).* • *(Sofas) can go.* • *Look! A (bath).* • *Which room?* • *Where is the (fridge)? In the (kitchen).* • *Not in the (kitchen).* • *Under the (bed).* • *Who's this?* • *Find the (mother).* • *Who's in the bedroom?* • *Yes, he's / she's (playing).* • *Hold up (the bathroom).* • *Well done!*

Vocabulary

House, bedroom, bathroom, living room, kitchen, bed, fridge, bath, sofa, playing, washing up, reading, brushing her teeth, in, under.

Activities

- Using non-linguistic aids (gestures, *flashcards*, objects, posters ...) to help comprehension and elicit responses.
- Eliciting non-linguistic responses in the classroom.
- Playing action games to consolidate the unit vocabulary.
- Playing with puppets to learn the parts of the house.
- Reciting, singing and acting out the chants and songs to learn the unit language.
- Playing the *Memory Game* with the rooms and their corresponding pieces of furniture.
- Miming different actions.
- Playing a guessing game *(Hide and Seek)* in pairs.
- Listening to sounds and matching them to the corresponding pictures.
- Playing while listening to a story in English.
- Using the picture dictionary.
- Completing the self-evaluation activity.
- Doing the evaluation activity at the end of the unit.

Attitudes

- Showing willingness to help out at home.
- Co-operating in keeping the class and the class materials tidy.
- Recognising the importance of caring about one's own health and hygiene.
- Participating willingly in class games and activities.
- Enjoying the songs, chants and stories in English.

CROSS-CURRICULAR THEMES

- **Non-sexism:** Helping pupils understand the importance of all the members of the family helping out at home and sharing the housework equally (Lesson 3: *Ending the lesson*).
- **Health education:** Showing pupils the importance of brushing one's teeth after each meal (Lesson 6: *Activity 1*).

EVALUATION CRITERIA

- Teacher's observation of attitude, effort and participation.
- Task Analysis: Oral comprehension (Lesson 6: *Beginning the lesson* - Following instructions; *Activity 1* - Listen and order). Oral expression (Lesson 6: *Activity 2* – My English dictionary). Answering questions for the teacher while doing the activities (Lesson 3: *Activity 2* - Memory Game; Lesson 4: *Activity 2* - Where?).
- Doing the self-evaluation activity.
- Completing the *Revision Sheet for Unit 4* (*Teacher's Guide*, page 101).

My clothes

GENERAL OBJECTIVES

- To learn clothes vocabulary.
- To understand the importance of being dressed in suitable clothes according to the season.

CONTENTS

Concepts

Functions

- To identify and name some articles of clothing.
- To identify colours: *purple* and *white*.
- To learn some Carnival vocabulary.
- To understand the word *old*.
- To revise vocabulary from previous units.
- To learn a traditional English party game.
- To understand a story in English.
- To learn new vocabulary from the picture dictionary.

Linguistic exponents

• Draw an old (chair). • If you are wearing a (jumper) you can go. • Jump on the table. • Run to the door. • What is it? • Who's wearing a (jumper)? • Look! A (dress). • Find the (dress). • What colour is the (shirt)? • Stick the (black and white hat) on (Banana). • Boys and girls. • Quiet please! • In the box, please. • Well done!

Vocabulary

T-shirt, shorts, jumper, hat, dress, shirt, trousers, shoes, hat, purple, white, magician, pirate, clown, mouse, chair, table, door, box, old, in, on, under, to.

Activities

- Using non-linguistic aids (gestures, *flashcards*, objects, posters ...) to help comprehension and elicit responses.
- Eliciting non-linguistic responses in the classroom.
- Doing drawing and colouring activities to develop motor skills.
- Miming different actions.
- Reciting, singing and acting out the chants and songs to learn the unit language.
- Repeating words from the unit to focus on pronunciation.
- Playing a guessing game to consolidate the unit vocabulary.
- Playing with puppets to learn the items of clothing.
- Using the poster to revise the vocabulary and structures.
- Playing a game with stickers to revise the vocabulary related to clothes and colours.
- Playing a guessing game while listening to a story in English.
- Playing a traditional party game.
- Consolidating the unit vocabulary with the help of the picture dictionary.
- Completing the self-evaluation activity.
- Doing the evaluation activity at the end of the unit.

Attitudes

- Recognising the importance of looking after one's health, and the importance of wearing the correct clothing depending on the weather.
- Showing interest in being polite to others by using *please* and *thank you* in the class.
- Participating willingly in class games and activities.
- Enjoying the songs, chants and stories in English.

CROSS-CURRICULAR THEMES

- **Health education:** Understanding the importance of being dressed in suitable clothes and shoes according to the weather (Lesson 2: *Beginning the lesson*).
- **Civic education:** Encouraging pupils to be polite by using *please* and *thank you* in the class (Lesson 5: *Developing the lesson*).

EVALUATION CRITERIA

- Teacher's observation of attitude, effort and participation.
- Task Analysis: Oral comprehension (Lesson 2: *Developing the lesson;* Lesson 3: *Beginning the lesson* - Following instructions; Lesson 4: *Developing the lesson* - Carnival costumes; Lesson 6: *Beginning the lesson* - Find). Oral Expression (Lesson 2: *Developing the lesson* - Who?). Class work (Lesson 4: *Developing the lesson* - Carnival costumes). Answering questions for the teacher while doing the activities (Lesson 2: *Developing the lesson* - Who?).
- Doing the self-evaluation activity.
- Completing the *Revision Sheet for Unit 5* (*Teacher's Guide*, page 102).

Farm animals

UNIT 6

GENERAL OBJECTIVES

- To learn the names of some farm and domestic animals.
- To recognise that animals are important for us and that we should respect and care for them.

CONTENTS

Concepts

Functions
- To learn the names of some farm and domestic animals.
- To identify animals from the noises they make.
- To learn the numbers *seven* and *eight*.
- To develop perception skills.
- To learn to ask how others are.
- To revise vocabulary from previous units.
- To understand a story in English.
- To learn new vocabulary from the picture dictionary.

Linguistic exponents
• What can you see / hear? • What's this? • What's (Chocolate) got? (Chocolate's) got a (dog). • Find the (horse). • How many (dogs)? • Be a (cow). • Run / jump / stop (rabbits)! • If you are wearing something (blue) (stand up). • Circle (number three). • Turn around. • How many (chicks) can you see? • How are you? I'm fine. • The (ball)'s not here. • There's / here's the (dog). • The (dog)'s got the ball.

Vocabulary
Cow, horse, pig, dog, cat, duck, sheep, chick, rabbit, ball, here, there.

Activities

- Using non-linguistic aids (gestures, *flashcards*, objects, noises ...) to help comprehension and elicit responses.
- Eliciting non-linguistic responses in the classroom.
- Doing a miming game to revise the vocabulary related to items of clothing.
- Reciting, singing and acting out the chants and songs to learn the unit language.
- Doing drawing, colouring and tracing activities to develop motor skills.
- Playing with puppets to learn the names of the animals and to ask how others are.
- Playing action games to revise the names of animals and vocabulary from previous units.
- Playing a guessing game with animal sounds.
- Predicting what is going to happen while listening to a story in English.
- Using the *poster* and cutout cards to revise the vocabulary.
- Consolidating the unit vocabulary with the help of the picture dictionary.
- Completing the self-evaluation activity.
- Doing the evaluation activity at the end of the unit.

Attitudes

- Recognising the importance of animals for the environment and for us and the importance of looking after them.
- Showing interest in doing the drawing and tracing activities well.
- Participating willingly in class games and activities.
- Enjoying the songs, chants and stories in English.

CROSS-CURRICULAR THEMES

- **Protection of the environment:** Helping pupils understand the importance of animals not only for the environment but also for us. Helping the pupils understand the importance of caring for them (Lesson 1: *Ending the lesson;* Lesson 6: *Beginning the lesson*).
- **Consumer education:** Focusing the children's attention on the fact that many products come from animals and the importance of such products, (milk, eggs, meat, wool, etc.) in our daily lives (Lesson 6: *Beginning the lesson*).

EVALUATION CRITERIA

- Teacher's observation of attitude, effort and participation.
- Task Analysis: Oral comprehension (Lesson 1: *Ending the lesson -* What's this?; Lesson 4: *Developing the lesson -* Say the numbers; *Ending the lesson -* How many?). Oral expression (Lesson 1: *Ending the lesson;* Lesson 4: *Developing the lesson -* Say the numbers; *Ending the lesson -* How many?). Class work (Lesson 1: *Ending the lesson -* Draw pets; Lesson 4: *Ending the lesson -* Matching activity). Answering questions for the teacher while doing the activities (Lesson 1: *Ending the lesson -* What's this?).
- Doing the self-evaluation activity.
- Completing the *Revision Sheet for Unit 6 (Teacher's Guide*, page 103).

Food

GENERAL OBJECTIVES

- To learn some food vocabulary.
- To understand the importance of eating in a healthy way.

CONTENTS

Concepts

Functions

- To identify and use some food vocabulary.
- To think about likes and dislikes regarding food.
- To learn the numbers *nine* and *ten*.
- To extract specific information from a listening text.
- To learn the new vocabulary and relate it to the language the children already know.
- To understand a story in English.
- To learn new vocabulary from the picture dictionary.

Linguistic exponents

• Who can you see? • Which fruit? • Who's in the bed? • How many (apples)? (Lemons) can go. • What's this? • Look! It's a (pear). • Mmm, (oranges). • Do you like ...? • I like / I don't like ... • What fruit do / don't you like? • I'm hungry (too). • Yum, yum! • Roll over! • Fall out.

Vocabulary

Fruit, apple, pear, orange, strawberry, lemon, banana, pizza, nine, ten, kite.

Activities

- Using non-linguistic aids (gestures, *flashcards*, objects, noises, posters, etc.) to help comprehension and elicit responses.
- Eliciting non-linguistic responses in the classroom.
- Doing a miming game to revise the vocabulary related to animals.
- Repeating words from the unit to focus on pronunciation.
- Playing a guessing game before listening to a recording.
- Playing with puppets and cards to learn the names of fruits.
- Reciting, singing and acting out chants and songs to learn the unit language.
- Doing a matching activity while listening to a text.
- Doing drawing, colouring and tracing activities to develop motor skills.
- Playing action games to follow instructions and revise vocabulary from previous units.
- Predicting what is going to happen while listening to a story in English.
- Acting out the story.
- Consolidating the unit vocabulary with the help of the picture dictionary.
- Completing the self-evaluation activity.
- Doing the evaluation activity at the end of the unit.

Attitudes

- Recognising both the importance and necessity of eating fresh fruit.
- Showing interest in pronouncing the new language correctly.
- Participating willingly in class games and activities.
- Enjoying the songs, chants and stories in English.

CROSS-CURRICULAR THEMES

- **Consumer education:** Stressing the importance of eating fresh fruit every day to be strong and healthy. (Lesson 1: *Developing the lesson;* Lesson 6: *Developing the lesson*).

EVALUATION CRITERIA

- Teacher's observation of attitude, effort and participation.
- Task Analysis: Oral expression (Lesson 1: *Beginning the lesson -* Guess the animal; Lesson 4: *Ending the lesson -* What fruit do you like?) Oral comprehension (Lesson 2: *Beginning the lesson -* Do you like?; Lesson 4: *Ending the lesson -* What fruit do you like?). Class work (Lesson 1: *Ending the lesson -* Which fruit?; Lesson 4: *Developing the lesson -* Matching activity). Answering questions for the teacher while doing the activities (Lesson 1: *Ending the lesson -* Which fruit?; Lesson 4: *Ending the lesson -* What fruit do you like?; Lesson 6: *Developing the lesson -* I like / I don't like).
- Doing the self-evaluation activity.
- Completing the *Revision Sheet for Unit 7* (*Teacher's Guide*, page 104).

UNIT 8

Let's play!

GENERAL OBJECTIVES

- To learn some vocabulary about toys.
- To learn some vocabulary about means of transport.
- To revise key language items learnt during the course.

CONTENTS

Concepts

Functions
- To identify and use some vocabulary about means of transport.
- To identify and use some vocabulary about toys.
- To differentiate the concepts *true* and *false*.
- To revise the vocabulary and structures from previous units.
- To learn new vocabulary and relate it to the language learnt previously.
- To understand a story in English.
- To learn new vocabulary from the picture dictionary.

Linguistic exponents
- *Where is (Banana)?* • *In the (car).* • *On the bike.*
- *Jump to the board for the (teddy bear).* • *Can you find the (ball)?* • *Find the (pigs).* • *Move your (feet) like a robot.* • *What's this number?* • *Stick the number (three) here.* • *Who is it?* • *It's party time!* • *(Banana)'s got a (ball).*

Vocabulary
Stop, go, up, down, yes, no, car, lorry, bike, teddy bear, ball, doll, robot, dance, come in, put, on, chocolate cake, balloons, party.

Activities

- Using non-linguistic aids (gestures, *flashcards*, objects, noises) to help comprehension and elicit responses.
- Eliciting non-linguistic responses in the classroom.
- Playing an action game using *stop* and *go* to introduce vocabulary related to means of transport.
- Playing a *True or false?* game.
- Playing a guessing game and a puppet game to revise toy vocabulary and vocabulary from previous units.
- Playing the *Memory Game* in pairs with the unit cutout cards.
- Saying or repeating words from the unit to focus on pronunciation.
- Doing a miming game to revise the vocabulary related to the parts of the body (*The Robot Game*).
- Playing a board game in pairs or small groups.
- Playing *Musical Cards*.
- Predicting what is going to happen while listening to a story in English.
- Answering questions about the story.
- Reciting, singing and acting out the chants and songs to revise the language learnt during the course.
- Consolidating the unit vocabulary with the help of the picture dictionary.
- Completing the self-evaluation activity.
- Doing the evaluation activity at the end of the unit.

Attitudes

- Understanding the importance of tidying up after working and playing.
- Showing interest in saying the new language correctly.
- Participating willingly in class games and activities.
- Enjoying the songs, chants and stories in English.
- Valuing one's own work positively.

CROSS-CURRICULAR THEMES

- **Non-sexism:** Recognising that all children can play with the same toys, both boys and girls. Recognising the value of enjoying oneself while playing together (Lesson 2: *Developing the lesson*).
- **Road safety:** Encouraging the pupils to pay attention and respect traffic signals, especially traffic lights. (Lesson 1: *Beginning the lesson*).

EVALUATION CRITERIA

- Teacher's observation of attitude, effort and participation.
- Task Analysis: Oral expression (Lesson 3: *Developing the lesson - Memory Game;* Lesson 4: *Developing the lesson -* Board Game; Lesson 5; *Beginning the lesson -* Musical Cards). Oral comprehension (Lesson 4; *Developing the lesson -* Robot Game). Class work (Lesson 4: *Developing the lesson -* Board Game). Answering questions for the teacher while doing the activities (Lesson 3: *Developing the lesson - Memory Game;* Lesson 4: Lesson 6: *Developing the lesson*).
- Doing the self-evaluation activity.
- Completing the *Revision Sheet for Unit 8 (Teacher's Guide,* page 105).

TEACHING PROGRAMME

Teaching notes

FUN ENGLISH

Hello

OBJECTIVES
- To learn the greetings *hello* and *goodbye*.
- To meet Banana and Chocolate.

LANGUAGE
Hello, goodbye. Banana, Chocolate.

RECEPTIVE LANGUAGE
Hello, I'm (Banana).

MATERIALS
Banana and Chocolate *flashcards*.

Beginning the lesson

- Start the lesson by saying: *Hello, I'm (your name),* waving as you do so to help comprehension. Encourage the children to say *hello* back to you.
- Hold up the *flashcards* of Banana and Chocolate and have them say: *Hello, I'm Banana / Chocolate.* Encourage the children to say *hello* to Banana and Chocolate.

Developing the lesson

- Tell the children they are going to listen to a chant with Banana and Chocolate, and that as they listen they should wave to Banana and Chocolate. Play the chant while holding up the *flashcards*.

R•1

Hello, hello, hello,
I'm Banana.
I'm Banana,
Hello, hello, hello.
Hello, hello, hello,
I'm Chocolate.
I'm Chocolate,
Hello, hello, hello.

- Play the chant again and encourage the children to join in.
- In L1 tell the children that Banana and Chocolate are going to sing, play and share their adventures with them in the English class, and that they will help them to learn lots of English.

Ending the lesson

- Have Banana and Chocolate leave the class. Hide the Banana and Chocolate *flashcards* behind your back or under the table and say: *Goodbye Banana, Goodbye Chocolate.* Invite the children to join in and say: *Goodbye!*

NOTE: Remind the children that they will need their passport size photo to make the puppet in the next lesson. You will also need a photo of yourself to be able to demonstrate the activity with the children.

Hello

OBJECTIVES
- To make the personalised puppet.
- To introduce yourself in English.

LANGUAGE
Hello, I'm ...

RECEPTIVE LANGUAGE
Open your books at page 12. Colour your puppets. Look! Cut, cut, cut! Fold and stick! Point to ...

MATERIALS
Scissors, glue, pencils, crayons, passport photos. Banana and Chocolate *flashcards*.

Beginning the lesson

- Using the Banana and Chocolate *flashcards* greet the children with *hello*.

- 🎧 Play the chant from lesson 1, encourage the children to join in, and at the same time to wave to Banana and Chocolate.

Developing the lesson

- Make sure the children have crayons, a pencil, scissors, glue and their photos (if the children have not yet brought their photo, let them draw their face in the space, they can stick their photo on when they bring it).

- Show the children page 12 in the *Pupil's Book* and say: *Open your books at page 12.* (Make this part of your class routine, always showing the page at the same time.) In L1 ask the children what they can see (a boy and a girl with puppets of themselves). Explain to the children that they are going to make puppets of themselves in the same way, to use throughout the year as they learn English.

- Demonstrate each stage of making the puppet with your own book and photo. Ask the children to go to page 11. The children first colour both sides of the puppet as they wish (again, explain that it will be a puppet of themselves, so they should colour the hair the same colour, draw clothes of their own, etc.). Say: *Colour your puppets.*

- Now show them how to cut out the whole page. Say: *Look! Cut, cut, cut!* Show them how to cut along the outline of the puppet and to fold and stick the two sides together. Say: *Fold and stick!* Finally the children stick on their photos where the head is.

- With your own puppet demonstrate to the class: *Hello, I'm (your name).* Encourage the children to do the same with each other. Show the children how to point with their puppets. Say: *Point to (Banana).* The children point to the Banana and Chocolate *flashcards* with their puppets.

Ending the lesson

- Hold up the Banana and Chocolate *flashcards* and let the children take it in turns to say *hello* and introduce themselves to Banana and Chocolate.

- Now tell the children they are going to learn a goodbye chant with Banana and Chocolate. Play the recording, as they listen have them move their puppets from side to side in a swaying fashion.

R·2 🎧

Goodbye, goodbye, goodbye, goodbye,
Goodbye, goodbye.
Goodbye, goodbye, goodbye, goodbye,
Goodbye, goodbye.

- Finally say *goodbye* with Banana and Chocolate. Encourage the children to do the same with their puppets.

- Collect in and store the children's puppets for future lessons.

My English class

LESSON 1

OBJECTIVES

- To understand and respond to the instructions *Stand up* and *Sit down*.
- To become familiar with the sounds of different people speaking in English.

RECEPTIVE LANGUAGE

Look! Who's this? What's your name? Stand up, sit down.

REVISION

Hello, I'm ... Goodbye.

MATERIALS

Banana and Chocolate *flashcards*. Some lively music. Pencils and crayons.

Beginning the lesson

- Teach the instructions *Stand up!* and *Sit down!* Put your chair in front of the class, sit on it and say: *Stand up!* standing up at the same time. Repeat with: *Sit down!* Get the children to join in as you say: *Stand up, sit down.* When the children are confident speed it up a little to make it fun.
- Using the Banana and Chocolate *flashcards*, say: *Hello, I'm (Banana).* to the children. Encourage the children to say *Hello, I'm ...* to Banana and Chocolate.
- Now use the *flashcards* to say to either yourself or a stronger pupil: *I'm (Banana). What's your name?* Encourage the child to reply: *I'm (Laura).* Continue with other children in the class.

Developing the lesson

ACTIVITY 1

- Show page 3 of the *Pupil's Book* and ask the children to open their books at this page. Point to the top of the page and, pointing at Banana, say: *Look! Who's this?* Elicit: *Banana.* Do the same for Chocolate. Then in L1 ask what they are doing (looking at Banana's photos).
- Now take the children to the other photos. Ask them to look carefully and to find Banana. Explain that these are Banana's holiday photos and ask them about the other characters, where they are, etc.

ACTIVITY 2

- Tell the children that they are going to listen to Banana interviewing the characters in the photos. Ask them to listen and follow. Say: *Listen to Banana.* Pause after each photo.

R•3 🎧

photo 1
Banana: Hello. I'm Banana. What's your name?
Ice cream seller: I'm Tom.
photo 2
Banana: Hello. I'm Banana. What's your name?
Boy: I'm Bob.
photo 3
Banana: Hello. I'm Banana. What's your name?
Rock star: I'm Nick. Yeah, yeah, yeah! I'm Nick, OK?

- Repeat the recording, this time as you pause after each photo ask: *Who's this?* Elicit: (1) *Tom*, (2) *Bob*, (3) *Nick*.

Ending the lesson

- 🎧 Play the *Goodbye* chant from the previous lesson (R – 2). Encourage the children to join in, waving at the same time.

Reinforcement activity

- Let the children sing the *Goodbye* chant again, this time let them hold hands and sway from left to right, like football supporters.

Extension activity

- Ask the children to sit in a circle on the floor and hand out the Banana and Chocolate *flashcards*. Play some lively music. The children pass the *flashcards* around in time to the music. When the music stops ask the child with Banana: *What's your name?* The child replies: *I'm Banana.* Do the same for Chocolate (you may prefer the children to use their own names).

Workbook   Page **3**

- Say: *Open your workbooks at page 3,* showing the page at the same time. Make sure they all have pencils and crayons. The children draw and colour a picture of themselves in the 'photo frame' with Banana and Chocolate.

My English class

OBJECTIVES
- To learn some classroom vocabulary.
- To learn the lesson chant.

LANGUAGE
Pencil, book, rubber, crayon.

RECEPTIVE LANGUAGE
Look! A (pencil). Very good. Who's this? Yes, the teacher, the teacher. Point to the (book).

MATERIALS
A pencil case with a rubber, a pencil, and a red crayon inside. The children's puppets. *Flashcards:* Banana, Chocolate, book, rubber, pencil, crayon.

Beginning the lesson

- Play *Chocolate Says* using the Chocolate *flashcard*. Say: *Chocolate says: stand up. Chocolate says: sit down.* The children listen and follow. When you say simply: *Stand up / sit down,* the children should remain still.

Developing the lesson

ACTIVITY 1
- Hold up the pencil case that you have prepared previously. In L1 ask the children what they think is inside. As they suggest different objects, draw them on the board.

- Now open the pencil case and take out each object, saying the name in English as you do so: *Look! (A pencil!)* If the object is already drawn on the board, put a circle round it. When you have taken out the three objects hold up each one and say the name again, this time the children repeat with you. Put a tick next to each object on the board as you do so, saying: *Very good.*

ACTIVITY 2
- Tell the children to open their *Pupil's Books* at pages 4 and 5. Have them look at the main picture and in L1 talk about what they can see. Point to the teacher and say: *Who's this?* When the children reply in L1 say: *Yes, the teacher, the teacher.* Point to the column on the left and say: *Look! (A pencil!)* Ask the children to find the pencil in the main picture. Then do the same for *crayon, rubber* and *teacher.*

- Point to the book in the column and say: *Look! A book!* The children repeat with you and then find the book in the main picture.

Ending the lesson

- Stick the *flashcards* of Banana and Chocolate on the board, and the following vocabulary *flashcards* underneath each one: Banana - pencil, rubber; Chocolate – crayon, book. Say: *Look! Banana's got a ...* Elicit: *pencil / rubber.* Do the same for Chocolate.

- Play the following chant and let the children listen or chant along; as they do so they should point to the *flashcards* on the board.

R•4 🎧

A pencil, a pencil,
Banana's got a pencil.
A crayon, a crayon,
Chocolate's got a crayon.
A rubber, a rubber,
Banana's got a rubber.
A book, a book,
Chocolate's got a book!

Reinforcement activity

- Stick the *flashcards* of the book, pencil, rubber and crayon around the room. Hand out the personalised puppets. The children listen and use their puppets to point to the objects. Say: *Point to the (book),* etc.

Extension activity

- Play *What's in the Bag?* Have a bag prepared with two of the following objects inside: pencil, crayon, rubber, book. Divide the class into two teams. Each team must guess which classroom objects are in your bag. Have a volunteer from each team come to the board and draw the two objects they have chosen. Finally take out the two objects, getting the class to name them. The team with the corresponding drawings wins.

Workbook   Page 4

- Say: *Open your workbooks at page 4.* Explain that Banana and Chocolate have got a problem, and that they are going to help them. The children look carefully at the page and match the two halves of each object together. Demonstrate with one of the objects. When they have finished go over the names of the objects they have found

KEY: book, crayon, pencil, rubber.

My English class

OBJECTIVES
- To learn the colours *green, red, blue, yellow* and *brown*.

LANGUAGE
Green, red, blue, yellow, brown. Yes, yes, yes! No, no, no!

RECEPTIVE LANGUAGE
Banana is yellow, (yes, yes, yes!) This is ... Find the colours! What colour?

REVISION
Rubber, crayon, book.

MATERIALS
Flashcards: Banana, Chocolate, green, red, blue, yellow, brown. A green rubber, a red crayon and a blue book. The children's puppets. Red, green, blue, yellow and brown crayons. Small pieces of paper.

Beginning the lesson

- 🎧 Start the lesson with the *Hello* chant from the Hello lesson (lesson 1, R – 1).

- Take out the yellow *flashcard* and say *Look! Yellow!* Then hold up Banana and say: *Banana is yellow.* Hold the two things together for the children to see the relation. Repeat for *brown* and *Chocolate*.

Developing the lesson

ACTIVITY 1
- Put the five colour *flashcards* across the board in the following order: yellow, brown, green, red, blue. Point to the first and say: *This is ...* Elicit: *Yellow*. Do the same for *brown*. Then point to the next *flashcard* and say: *Green. This is green.* Repeat for the other two colours. Now point to one of the flashcards at random and say: *This is ...* eliciting the colour from the class. Do this several times until you feel the children are confident with the colours.

ACTIVITY 2
- Say: *Open your books at page 5.* Take the children to the column on the right and go through the colours *(green, red, blue, yellow, brown)*.

- **EVALUATION:** Explain to the children that they have to find these colours in the main picture. Say: *Find the colours!* As the children work go round and ask: *What colour?* The children should point to the things they have found and tell you the colour. Use this as an opportunity to evaluate the work of four or five of the children.

Ending the lesson

- Hold up the Banana *flashcard* and say: *Banana is yellow, yes, yes, yes!* nodding your head as you do so, to convey the meaning. Do the same for the other objects with their corresponding colours (Chocolate – brown; rubber – green; crayon – red; book – blue). Encourage the children to join in with *Yes, yes, yes!*

- Now hold up the Banana *flashcard* and say: *Banana is brown. No, no, no!*, shaking your head to indicate negation. Encourage the children to join in saying: *No, no, no!* Hold up Chocolate and say: *Chocolate is brown.* The children say: *Yes, yes, yes!* Repeat with the green rubber, red crayon and blue book.

- Now play the following chant. Encourage the children to join in with the affirmations and the negations:

R•5 🎧

Banana is yellow. Yes, yes, yes!
Chocolate is yellow. No, no, no!
Chocolate is brown. Yes, yes, yes!
Banana is brown. No! No! No!

Reinforcement activity

- Hand out the children's personalised puppets and take the children to pages 4 and 5 of the *Pupil's Book.* Say: *Point to (yellow).* The children use their puppets to find and point to the colours in the main picture.

Extension activity

- An adaptation of the previous activity. This time the children listen and point with their personalised puppets to particular objects in the main picture. Say: *Point to the green rubber, point to the blue book,* etc.

Workbook   Page 5

- Say: *Open your workbooks at page 5.* Ask the children to look at the page and to tell you what they are going to do (play *Bingo*). Make sure the children have green, blue, red, yellow and brown crayons. Tell the children to colour in the four 'patches' as they choose.

- When the children are ready, play *Bingo*. First hand out the small pieces of paper and ask the children to cover two objects and two colours. At random, name the colours and objects on the page. Using a pencil, the children tick off those that they have on their Bingo 'card'. The first child to have a complete card raises their hand and says: *Bingo!* Go through all the colours and objects so that everyone finishes the game.

My English class

LESSON 4

OBJECTIVES
- To learn the numbers one to four.
- To learn the unit song.

LANGUAGE
Up, down, one, two, three, four. Chair.

RECEPTIVE LANGUAGE
Let's count! Look! One chair. Close your books. Let's sing! Show me (blue). Colour number one (blue). What number is (red?) What colour is (two)?

REVISION
Crayon, book, rubber.

MATERIALS
Prepared cards with the numbers one to four. A crayon, two chairs, three rubbers and four books (to practise the song). Red, blue, green and yellow crayons.

Beginning the lesson

- Hold up the cards of the numbers one to four, or write these numbers on the board. *Say: Let's count! One. Two. Three. Four.* Repeat with the children counting.

- Bring your chair to the front of the class and introduce *chair* saying: *Look! A chair.* Now show the following objects in the following order: one crayon, two chairs, three rubbers, four books. Say: *One crayon, two chairs, three rubbers, four books.* Each time you do so encourage the children to repeat each phrase.

Developing the lesson

ACTIVITY 1
- Say: *Open your books at page 6.* Ask the children what they can see *(1 crayon, 2 chairs, 3 rubbers, 4 books).* Ask them to find Banana and Chocolate and to tell you what they are doing (they are stretching up and down). Practise this stretching with the children. Say: *Up!* The children should stretch up as high as they can. Say: *Down!* The children bend over to try and touch their toes. Encourage the children to repeat the words and actions. Say: *Close your books,* closing your own at the same time so the children can see what to do.

- Have the items from the song ready at the front of the class in the following order, from left to right (your right to left): 1 crayon, 2 chairs, 3 rubbers, 4 books. Say: *Let's sing!*

ACTIVITY 2
- Play the song. As the children listen point to each object or group of objects as they 'appear' in the song. At the end of each line of the song, stretch up, and then down.

- Repeat the song and have the children do the actions with you. Play the song as many times as you feel necessary and encourage the children to sing along.

R·6

Chorus:

Tra la la la la,
Tra la la la la.
Tra la la la la,
Tra la la la la.

One crayon, one crayon!
Up, down.
One crayon, one crayon!
Up, down.

(chorus)

One crayon, two chairs!
Up, down.
One crayon, two chairs!
Up, down.

(chorus)

One crayon, two chairs, three rubbers!
Up, down.
One crayon, two chairs, three rubbers!
Up, down.

(chorus)

One crayon, two chairs, three rubbers, four books!
Up, down.
One crayon, two chairs, three rubbers, four books!
Up, down.

(chorus)

Ending the lesson

- **EVALUATION:** Go back to page 6 of the *Pupil's Book* and hand out red, blue, green and yellow crayons. Say: *Show me (blue). Colour number one (blue),* holding up your book and pointing as you do so. Do the same with the rest of the numbers (2 – green; 3 – red; 4 – yellow). As they are working, go round the class and ask: *What number is (red?) What colour is (two)?* etc. Use this as an opportunity to evaluate the progress of several children.

Reinforcement activity

- Play the following game. Using the previous colouring activity for reference, say: *One.* The children say: *Blue.* Say: *Yellow.* The children say: *Four,* etc.

Extension activity

- Go back to page 6 of the *Pupil's Book.* Now describe the objects with both number and colour. Say: *Look! One red crayon, two yellow chairs,* etc. Point to the objects and elicit them from the children with the colour and number.

Workbook
Page **6**

- Say: *Open your workbooks at page 6.* In the first activity the children match the numbers with the corresponding objects. In the second, they follow the footsteps from the objects to the number and then trace over the numbers.

My English class

LESSON 5

OBJECTIVES
- To enjoy listening to a story in English.
- To recognise the importance of helping others when they are in need.

RECEPTIVE LANGUAGE
Be (happy!) Chocolate isn't brown. Mix, mix, mix! (Blue) and (yellow) make (green). Chocolate is happy.

REVISION
Red, yellow, blue, green, brown.

MATERIALS
Chocolate *flashcard*. Red, blue and yellow paints. Photocopies of the Resource Sheet on page 78 of the *Resource Bank*.

Beginning the lesson

- 🎧 Play the chant from lesson 3 (R – 5) encouraging the children to join in. Finally say: *Banana is ...* Elicit: *Yellow*. Then say: *Chocolate is ...* and elicit: *Brown*.

- Tell the children it's time for a story. Have them come and sit round you in a semi-circle if possible, or take them to the reading corner if you have one.

Developing the lesson

ACTIVITY 1
- Point to the picture at the top of page 7 of the *Pupil's Book* and explain that granny is telling a story to Banana and Chocolate. Then ask them to look at the first picture of the story and ask what they can see (Banana and Chocolate are sad. Banana is yellow, but Chocolate isn't brown). Say: *Banana and Chocolate are sad,* exaggerating a sad expression. Point out the paints that the three children have. Elicit the colours of the paints *(red, yellow* and *blue)*. Ask the children what they think the children are going to do (paint Chocolate). Establish the fact that there is no brown paint.

ACTIVITY 2
- Tell the story, following the indications below. After each scene ask the children what they think will happen next.

R•7 🎧

Chocolate is brown

picture 1
Narrator:
The children have got yellow paint, and red paint and blue paint. Banana is yellow. Chocolate is ... Chocolate isn't brown. The children have no brown paint! Oh dear.
/Shake your head to indicate the negation here, and look sad./

picture 2
Look! Mix, mix, mix. Mix, mix, mix, mix. /Indicate a mixing motion with your arm./
Blue and yellow make ... green.
Mix, mix, mix. Mix, mix, mix.

And green and red make BROWN!
picture 3
The children paint Chocolate brown! /Indicate a painting motion./

picture 4
Look! Now Chocolate is happy!
Chocolate: Yipeee! /Exaggerate a 'happy' face./

- Tell the story again or listen using the recording. This time the children carry out the actions with you:

  Picture 1 – Express the negation of 'Banana isn't brown'. Exaggerate the sad expression.
  Picture 2 – The children mime mixing the paint.
  Picture 3 – The children mime painting.
  Picture 4 – The children jump up and down shouting 'Yipeee!' with exaggerated 'happy' faces.

- Explain to the class that the children helped Chocolate when he was sad, and that he is now happy. Point out the importance of helping others when in need.

Ending the lesson

- Tell the children it's the end of the story, but that there will be many more throughout the year. Play the *End of the story* song (which is recorded at the end of each story) and encourage the children to sing along:

R ● THE END OF THE STORY SONG 🎧

It's the end of the story,	It's the end of the story,
It's the end, it's the end.	It's the end, it's the end.
It's the end of the story,	It's the end of the story,
It's the end, it's the end.	It's the end, it's the end.

Reinforcement activity

- Use the Chocolate *flashcard* to play *Chocolate Says* with the instructions: *Be happy!* and *Be sad!*

Extension activity

- Use red, yellow and blue paints to show the children how they can first make green, and then brown. Once they have mixed the paints hand out the Resource sheet from page 78. The children complete the sheet to show how the colours are formed.

NOTE: Tell the children that they will need to bring a large envelope to class for the following lesson to store their flashcards in.

Workbook   Page 7

- Say: *Open your workbooks at page 7.* The children first order the pictures from the story in the correct order from 1 – 4. They then find the two pictures of Banana and Chocolate which are the same.

My English class

LESSON 6

OBJECTIVES
- To revise and consolidate the key language from the unit.
- To provide an opportunity for the children to reflect on the things they have done in this unit

RECEPTIVE LANGUAGE
Jump! Take a star and stick it here!

REVISION
The key language from unit 1.

MATERIALS
Scissors. Large envelopes to store the cutout cards. The star stickers (one per child). Photocopies of the *Revision Sheet for Unit 1* (see *Evaluation* page 98).

Beginning the lesson

- Ask the children about the story from the previous lesson, see how much they can tell you. Revise the colours. Say: *Yellow and blue make ...* Elicit: *Green.* Say: *Green and red make ...* Elicit: *Brown.*
- Now teach the command *Jump!* Say: *Stand up! Sit down! Stand up! Jump!*, showing the children what to do. Repeat several times until the children are confident.

Developing the lesson

ACTIVITY 1
- Hand out the scissors and tell the children they are going to cut out some cards. Show the children the page and say: *Open your books at page 9.* Show the children how to first cut out the whole page, and then the individual cards. Have the children put their names on the back of each.
- When the children are ready, play card game 3, on page 77 of the *Resource Bank.*

ACTIVITY 2
- 🎧 Now play the song from lesson 4 (R - 6). The children work in groups of four. They should work together and place the following number of cutout cards on their desks: 1 crayon, 2 chairs, 3 rubbers and 4 books. As they listen to the song the children hold up the corresponding cards.
- Take the children to their **My English dictionary** on page 8. In L1 explain that all the things they have learnt in this unit are here. Go through them with the children and have them repeat after you. Alternatively they can listen to the recording and repeat, following in their books.

R•8 🎧
- Banana, Chocolate.
- Pencil, book, crayon, rubber.
- Teacher.
- Blue, green, red, brown, yellow.
- One crayon, two crayons, three crayons, four crayons.
- Chair.

- **SELF-EVALUATION:** Tell the children they have worked well in this unit, say: *Well done!* Show the children their stickers and point out the stars. Say: *Take a star and stick it here!* Point to *Yaka Boo!* on the dictionary page and have the children stick their star at the end of Banana's wand. Now play the *Yaka Boo!* chant, which is recorded at the end of every English dictionary recording.

R • THE YAKA BOO! CHANT 🎧

Yaka Boo!
Yaka Boo!
A star for me,
A star for you!
Goodbye!

Ending the lesson

- Ask the children to put their cards away carefully in their envelopes and to bring the envelopes to the front. Write the children's names on each one and store them for future lessons.

END OF UNIT EVALUATION

- Hand out the photocopies of the *Revision Sheet for Unit 1*, which can be found on page 98. The indications on how to carry out the evaluation are outlined on page 94.

Workbook   Page 8

- Say: *Open your workbooks at page 8.* Make sure the children have crayons of the five colours they have learnt. Take them to the 'patches' at the top of the page and say: *Colour number one yellow, colour number two blue, colour number three red, colour number four green.* The children then colour the parachute according to the colour code, and finally colour Banana and Chocolate yellow and brown.

My body

OBJECTIVES
- To learn vocabulary related to the face.

LANGUAGE
Eyes, mouth, nose.

RECEPTIVE LANGUAGE
Look, look, look! Witch. Run! Touch (Chocolate's) (nose). Show me your (eyes). Green eyes can go.

REVISION
Who's this? Yes. No.

MATERIALS
Prepared number cards one to four. Banana and Chocolate *flashcards.*

Beginning the lesson

- Warm up the class with the stretching activity from the previous unit. Say: *Up!* The children stretch their arms up as high as they can. Say: *Down!* The children bend over and touch their toes. Then add: *Run!* and show the children how to run on the spot. Repeat these actions several times.

- Introduce the words *eyes, nose* and *mouth* with the Banana and Chocolate *flashcards.* Hold up Banana and say: *Look! Eyes, nose, mouth.* Repeat with Chocolate. Now invite individual children to come to the front and touch. Say: *Touch Chocolate's nose. Touch Banana's mouth,* etc.

- Finally have the class touch parts of their own face. Say: *Touch your (eyes),* etc.

Developing the lesson

ACTIVITY 1
- Say: *Open your books at page 13.* Ask: *Who's this?* pointing to Banana. Repeat for Chocolate and then the witch. Say: *Yes, a witch. A witch!* In L1 tell the children that Banana and Chocolate have come across a witch, and that they are very frightened. They are looking at the witch's face. Tell the children to look closely at the witch's face and point as they listen to Banana and Chocolate:

 R•9

Banana: Look, look, look!
Two eyes! Two eyes!

Chocolate: Look, look, look!
One nose! One nose!

Banana: Look, look, look!
One mouth! One mouth!

Witch: Booooooooooooooo!

Banana and Chocolate: Agghh! A witch!

ACTIVITY 2
- Let the children listen a second time and chant the parts of the face, carrying out the following actions (show them how to do it first):

    eyes – the children blink several times
    nose – the children wiggle their noses
    mouth – the children cup their hands around their mouths.

- Finally the children pretend to run away!

Ending the lesson

- Say: *Show me your eyes. Show me your nose. Show me your mouth.* The children listen and touch the parts of their face. Now touch your own eyes and say: *Nose?* Encourage the children to shout *No.* Touch your nose and say: *Eyes?* Again the children shout *No.* Repeat to elicit both *Yes* and *No* from the children.

- Group the children according to their eye colour (brown, green, blue, etc.). Say: *(Green) eyes can go! Goodbye (green) eyes.* Repeat with the other colours.

Reinforcement activity

- Play *Chocolate Says,* using *Touch your eyes / nose / mouth.*

Extension activity

- Play the *Witches Game.* This should ideally be played outside in the playground. The children form two lines, 'witches' and 'children', starting from 'home'. Have the number cards 1 to 4 turned face down. Chose a card at random and say the number. The 'children' take that many steps forward, counting as they do so. Repeat for the 'witches'. As the two lines get closer to each other decide the moment to shout: *A witch! Run!* The witches should chase and try to catch the children, who at the same time try to return 'home'. Those children caught become 'witches' and form part of the witches line. The game continues until all the children have been caught.

orkbook   Page **9**

- Say: *Open your workbooks at page 9.* Ask: *Who's this?* for each character. Establish that they are all missing a part of the face. The children complete the faces in their books. As they work, go round and elicit from the children the parts they are drawing.

    KEY: Banana – eyes; Witch – nose; Chocolate – mouth.

My body

LESSON 2

OBJECTIVES
- To learn the colours *black* and *orange*.
- To learn vocabulary related to Halloween.

LANGUAGE
Black, orange, witch, monster, cat, ghost, pumpkin.

RECEPTIVE LANGUAGE
How many (witches)? Ghost, cat, monster, pumpkin. Look and find.

REVISION
The numbers one to four. *What colour? Red, blue, yellow, green, brown.* Classroom objects.

MATERIALS
Personalised puppets. *Flashcards:* witch, ghost, monster, pumpkin, cat, black, orange, yellow, brown, red, blue, green. Black and orange crayons.

Beginning the lesson

- Start the lesson with the chant from the previous lesson (R – 9). The children carry out the actions as they listen.

Developing the lesson

ACTIVITY 1
- Ask the children what they can remember about Banana and Chocolate from the previous lesson and where they think Banana and Chocolate are now. Tell the children that they are at a Halloween party with the witch and some other characters. Stick the *flashcards* on the board in the following order: witch, monster, cat, ghost, pumpkin. Say: *Look! A witch. A monster. A cat. A ghost. A pumpkin.* Encourage the children to repeat the words after you. Then write the number one underneath each. Ask: *How many witches?* Elicit from the children: *One (witch),* etc.

- Tell the children they are going to look at a picture of the Halloween party and count the witches, monsters, cats, ghosts and pumpkins. Say: *Open your books at pages 14 and 15. Look and find!* Give the children a few minutes to look at the picture. Then go back to the *flashcards* on the board and ask the children to tell you what they have found (1 witch, 1 monster, 2 cats, 3 ghosts and 4 pumpkins). Write the corresponding numbers underneath the *flashcards* on the board.

ACTIVITY 2
- **EVALUATION:** Take the orange *flashcard* and hold it up for the children to see. Say: *Look! Orange.* Now repeat with *black.* Encourage the children to repeat the words after you. Make sure the children have black and orange crayons. Hold up a black crayon and say: *Look! Black. Colour the cats black!* Then hold up an orange crayon and say: *Look! Orange. Colour the pumpkins orange!* As the children work in their *Pupil's Books,* go round and ask: *What colour?* Elicit:

Black or *orange.* Use this as an opportunity to evaluate the progress of several children.

- Now play the chant. The children listen and point in their books. Play the chant again and have the children join in.

R•10

Orange pumpkins, orange pumpkins, Black cats! Black cats!	Orange pumpkins, orange pumpkins, Black cats! Black cats!

Ending the lesson

- Stick the seven colour *flashcards* on the board. Give the children a few minutes to find things in the room which correspond to those colours. Hand out the personalised puppets. Say: *Point to (red),* etc. The children point to the red object(s) they have identified in the classroom with their puppet. If you have the space you could alternatively do this activity with the children running to the different colours. Say: *Run to (red),* etc.

Reinforcement activity

- Divide the class into four groups: monsters, cats, ghosts and witches. Let the children decide first in their groups how they will mime their character. Then shout out the character names at random, the children listen and mime when they hear their character. Speed up as the children become more confident.

Extension activity

- Put the seven colour *flashcards* on the board again. Challenge the children by saying the name of an object, they should shout out the colour. Say: *Cat,* the children reply: *Black.* Use Banana, Chocolate, the monster, the pumpkin, the witch, and different objects in the class (pencil, chair, book, crayon, rubber).

Workbook   Page 10

- Say: *Open your workbooks at page 10.* The children find and circle the differences between the two pictures. (1st picture – 2 cats, 2 ghosts, the witch, the monster, 4 pumpkins; 2nd picture – 3 cats, 2 ghosts but one without a mouth, the monster but without a nose, 3 pumpkins but one without eyes.) As the children work, go round and elicit the differences they have found.

My body

OBJECTIVES

- To learn vocabulary related to the body.

LANGUAGE

Arms, hands, legs, feet.

RECEPTIVE LANGUAGE

How many (arms)? Touch your partner's (hands). Hold hands! Arms up! Find the monster.

REVISION

Action verbs. *Who's this?*

MATERIALS

Personalised puppets. Sheets of paper and crayons. *Halloween poster*.

Beginning the lesson

- Do the following warm up routine with the children. Say: *Stand up! Run! Jump! Sit down!* Repeat several times, finishing with *Stand up!*

- Shake your arms and say: *Look! Arms!* Get the children to shake their arms and hold them up in the air. Now shake your hands and say: *Look! Hands!* The children copy you. Do the same with *legs*, and finally *feet*. Each time encourage the children to repeat the words after you.

- Now simply name the parts of the body. The children listen and shake the corresponding body part as they hear it. Say: *Legs! Hands! Arms! Feet!*, etc.

Developing the lesson

- Ask the children to open their *Pupil's Books* at pages 14 and 15. Ask them about Banana and Chocolate, what they are doing, how they feel, etc.

- Hold up your own book and point to the witch. Ask: *Who's this?* Elicit: *A witch.* Repeat for the ghost and then the monster. Now take the children to the column on the right of the page. Say: *Look! Hands! Arms! Legs! Feet!* Then ask the children to find the parts of the body in the main picture (they all belong to the monster).

- Finally draw an outline of the monster's head and body on the board and ask the children: *How many (arms)?* Encourage the children to look at the monster in their books and to answer. Invite children to come and draw the parts on the monster. Repeat for *feet, legs, hands, eyes, nose* and *mouth*.

Ending the lesson

- Divide the class into pairs and hand out the personalised puppets. The children listen and touch the parts of the body on their partner with the puppet. Say: *Touch your partner's (hands),* etc.

- 🎧 Play the *Goodbye* chant from the Hello lesson (lesson 2, R - 2). Let the children sing along holding hands and swaying their arms. Say: *Hold hands! Arms up!*

Reinforcement activity

- Put up the *Halloween poster*. Now give instructions to the children. Say: *Find the witch. Find the monster,* etc.

Extension activity

- Do a monster dictation. Hand out sheets of paper and crayons to the children. Tell them they are going to draw a monster but that they must listen to your instructions. Indicate that they should first draw the head and the body. Do this on the board for them to copy. Then say: *The monster's got ... (three) (legs),* etc. When the children have finished let them compare their drawings before drawing the original version on the board.

Workbook   Page **11**

- Say: *Open your workbooks at page 11.* The children find the missing parts of the witch, cat and monster's bodies and then join them together with a line.

My body

OBJECTIVES
- To learn the unit song.
- To make a skeleton cutout.

LANGUAGE
Skeleton.

REVISION
Parts of the body.

MATERIALS
Halloween poster. Photocopies of the skeleton template (page 79 of the *Resource Bank*). A prepared skeleton. Scissors. *Flashcards:* the Halloween characters plus the seven colours learnt so far.

Beginning the lesson

- Put up the *poster* and tell the children they are going to meet somebody else from the Halloween party today. Invite the children to guess who it might be. When they guess correctly say: *Very good, the skeleton.* Take out your own prepared skeleton. Shake the skeleton around. Get the children to say the word after you. Then point to the parts of the body the children already know and elicit the names from the children. Tell the children that in today's lesson they are going to learn a song about the skeleton, and to make one too.

Developing the lesson

ACTIVITY 1
- Say: *Open your books at page 16.* Ask the children what they can see (a skeleton dancing). Tell the children the skeleton is dancing to his song. Play the song. First have the children listen and watch you point to the different parts of your own body.

R•11 🎧

Chorus:
I'm a skeleton, crick crack, crick crack.
I'm a skeleton, crick crack, crick crack.

Two feet - crick, crack,
Two feet - crick, crack.
Two legs - crick, crack,
Two legs - crick, crack.

(Chorus)

Two arms - crick, crack,
Two arms - crick, crack.
Two hands - crick, crack,
Two hands - crick, crack.

(Chorus)

Two eyes - tick, tack,
One nose,
One mouth.

I'm a skeleton, crick crack, crick crack.
I'm a skeleton, CRICK, CRACK, CRICK, CRACK!
CRRRRRAAAAAAACKKKKKKK!

- Play the song again. This time ask the children to stand up and do the actions, moving the appropriate parts of their body, and singing along.

ACTIVITY 2
- **EVALUATION:** Hand out the photocopies of the skeleton template and the scissors. Tell the children they are going to make a skeleton by cutting out the parts on the right of the page and sticking them in the correct place. (Note: if you are using the *Workbook* you will find the activity on page 13). As the children make the skeletons go round and elicit the parts of the body that they have learnt. Use this as an opportunity to evaluate the progress of several children.
- Finally sing the song again. The children indicate the parts of the body on their skeletons.

Ending the lesson

- Finish the lesson with the tracing activity at the bottom of page 16. As the children work, go round the class and ask the children to name the numbers they are working on.

Reinforcement activity

- Say: *Stand up!* Play *Race the Teacher*. Give the children the following instructions, they should try and do them before you can. Say: *Touch your feet, touch your eyes, touch your nose, touch your hands, touch your legs, touch your arms, touch your mouth. Sit down!*

Extension activity

- Divide the class into two teams, ghosts and monsters. Use the Halloween and colours *flashcards*. Show a card very quickly, the first child to shout the correct word wins a point for their team.

My body

OBJECTIVES

- To enjoy listening to a story in English.
- To reinforce the importance of helping others when in difficulty.

LANGUAGE

Big, small.

Beginning the lesson

- Say: *Stand up! Run! Jump! Be big!* Show the children how to open out their arms, legs, and even cheeks, to make a big shape. Repeat the instructions. Then say: *Run! Jump! Be small!* Show the children how to crouch down into a ball, making a small shape. Repeat.

- Tell the children it's time for a story, and to come and sit round you in a semi-circle.

Developing the lesson

- Show granny at the top of page 17 of the *Pupil's Book*. Tell the children they are going to listen to a story about Banana and Chocolate and the witch!

- Point to the first picture and ask the children what they can see (Banana and Chocolate at school, the witch has just entered the classroom and has cast a spell). Ask for suggestions from the children as to what they think is going to happen next.

- Tell the story, pausing after each picture and inviting the children to predict what will happen next.

R•12

The witch!

picture 1:
Banana and Chocolate: Oh, look! The witch!
Witch: Ha, ha, ha!
Abracadabra!

picture 2:
Chocolate: Oh no Banana! Look! You're small! I'm big and you're small!
Banana: Oh dear, I'm small. You're big, Chocolate, and I'm small!
Chocolate: I'm big, and the witch is big. But you're small. Oh dear!

picture 3:
Witch: Ha, ha, ha!
Banana: Oh dear! I'm small.
Chocolate is big, and I'm small.

picture 4:
Chocolate: Abracadabra!
Witch: Oh no, I'm small! I'm small!
Banana: And we are big! We are big!
Chocolate: Ha, ha, ha!

- Ask the children if they can tell you the magic word which made Banana small, and then big again *(Abracadabra)*. Tell the story again, or use the recording. Then act out the story with the children. Divide the class into three groups to play the roles of Banana, Chocolate and the witch. Use the following adapted script and actions:

  Witch: *Abracadabra!*
  /The witches move their arm in a gesture of casting a spell with a wand/
  Banana: *I'm small! I'm small!*
  /The Bananas crouch down into a ball/
  Witch: *Ha, ha, ha, ha, ha! He, he, he, he, he!*
  /The witches clutch at their stomachs as they laugh/
  Chocolate: *Abracadabra!*
  /The Chocolates move their arm as if casting a spell with a wand/
  Banana: *I'm big! I'm big!*

Ending the lesson

- Play the *End of the story* song, which follows the story recording, and encourage the children to sing along.

- Say goodbye to the class and let the children go according to their roles in the story, say: *Goodbye witches. Goodbye Bananas. Goodbye Chocolates.*

Reinforcement activity

- Go round the class allocating the numbers from one to four to the children. Now give the following instructions, and explain to the children that they should only respond if they hear their number. Say: *Be (happy)! Number threes. Be (big)! Number ones,* etc.

Extension activity

- Draw a monster on the board with four of the following: legs, arms, hands, feet, eyes, noses, eyes. The children come to the front and remove parts of the body as you instruct. Say: *Rub out (two eyes),* etc.

**orkbook**   Page **12**

- Say: *Open your workbooks at page 12.* First the children try to find Banana and Chocolate (Banana is in the pumpkin, Chocolate is behind a tree). They then draw themselves at the Halloween party.

My body

LESSON 6

OBJECTIVES
- To revise and consolidate the key language from the unit.
- To provide an opportunity for the children to reflect on the things they have done in this unit.

RECEPTIVE LANGUAGE
Let's play the poster quiz. Hold up (the witch). Show me Banana and Chocolate big.

MATERIALS
Halloween poster. Scissors. The children's card envelopes. The star stickers (one per child). Photocopies of *Revision Sheet for Unit 2* (see *Evaluation* page 99).

Beginning the lesson

- Put up the *poster* and play the *Poster quiz*. Say: *Let's play the poster quiz*. Make true and false statements about the poster for the children. If they are true the children should stand up, if they are false the children remain seated.

  1) *There are three cats in the poster.* (F)
  2) *There are four pumpkins in the poster.* (T)
  3) *The monster is brown.* (T)
  4) *The skeleton has got two arms.* (T)
  5) *The monster has got four legs.* (F)
  6) *Banana is yellow.* (T)
  7) *Chocolate is orange.* (F)
  8) *Banana and Chocolate are black.* (F)

Developing the lesson

ACTIVITY 1
- Hand out the scissors and ask the children to turn to page 19 in their *Pupil's Books*. The children prepare the cutout cards as indicated in the previous unit. Remind the children to write their names on the back of each one. When the children are ready go through each card, say: *Hold up the witch. Show me Banana and Chocolate big,* etc. Now play the card game 4 on page 77 of the *Resource Bank*.

ACTIVITY 2
- Take the children to **My English dictionary** on page 18. Play the recording of the vocabulary, the children listen and point in their books. Then go through the pictures again and elicit the language from the children.

R•13

- Eyes, nose, mouth, hands, arms, legs, feet.
- Black, orange.

- Tell the children they have worked well in this unit and show them their gold stars. Say: *Take a star and stick it here*, pointing to the end of Banana's magic wand on page 18. Then play the *Yaka Boo!* chant that follows the English dictionary recording, and encourage the children to join in.

Ending the lesson

- Hand out the children's envelopes so they can store their cutout cards. It is useful to encourage the children to clip each set together with a paper clip to help keep them organised.

END OF UNIT EVALUATION
- Hand out the photocopies of the *Revision Sheet for Unit 2*, which can be found on page 99. The indications on how to carry out the evaluation are outlined on page 94.

My family

LESSON 1

OBJECTIVES
- To identify the members of Banana's family.
- To learn the unit chant.

LANGUAGE
Family, father, mother, brother, sister, baby.

RECEPTIVE LANGUAGE
This is my (mother). Smile!

REVISION
Halloween vocabulary, parts of the body.

MATERIALS
Banana and Chocolate *flashcards*. A set of Banana family cutout cards from the *Pupil's Book* page 27. Crayons of the seven colours the children have learnt so far.

Beginning the lesson

- Say the following Halloween characters and have the children mime each one: *Witch, ghost, monster, skeleton* and *cat*. Divide the class into five corresponding groups and play *Chocolate Says*. Say: *Chocolate says: touch your (nose) (witches)! Touch your (mouth) (cats)!* Revise the parts of the body which the children learnt in the previous lesson.

Developing the lesson

ACTIVITY 1
- Take the Banana *flashcard* and say: *Hello!*. Encourage the children to reply: *Hello Banana*. Tell the children that Banana has been taking more photos, this time of his family, and that he would like to show them to the children. Before you show the family cutout cards, ask the children who they think Banana has photos of. Then have Banana take the cards, one by one, to present his family to the children. Say: *Look children, this is my (father)*. Do the same for the rest of the family.

- Ask the children to open their *Pupil's Books* at page 21. Give the children a few minutes to look at the page and then say: *Look! Banana's family. Find Banana*. Ask the children what he is doing (taking photos, but standing on his hand at the same time!). Then say: *Point to the (father)*, etc. The children listen and point to the different family members. Finally ask the children what is unusual or different about the father (he's got a plaster cast on his leg). Ask the children how they think it happened. Don't explain yet, leave this for the children to see for themselves in this unit's story.

ACTIVITY 2
- Tell the children that Banana is going to chant about his family. Ask the children to listen and point to the members of the family as they hear them.

R•14

Hello, hello!
This is my father,
This is my mother.
This is my sister,

And this is my brother.
This is the baby,
And this is me!
Me, and my family!

- Play the chant again and encourage the children to join in.

Ending the lesson

- Ask the children to take part in Banana's family photo and arrange them at the front of the class as if they were having their photo taken. Pretend to take a photo. Say: *Smile!* Continue until all the children have had a chance to be in the Banana family photo. They can also take turns at taking the photo.

Reinforcement activity

- Take the children back to page 21 in their *Pupil's Books*. Give instructions and while the children listen they draw a circle around the corresponding person. First show them what to do by sticking the family cards on the board and drawing a circle round each one as you say: *Draw a circle round the (father)*, etc.

Extension activity

- Repeat the reinforcement activity, but this time in your instructions give the colour they should use. Say: *Draw a (blue) circle round the mother*, etc.

Workbook   Page 15

- Say: *Open your workbooks at page15*. Ask the children to find Chocolate (at the bottom of the page on the right). Tell the children that they are going to draw Chocolate's family, they should decide which frame to put the father, mother, brother, sister and baby in. As the children work go round asking the children who the different family members are and why they have drawn them where they have.

My family

LESSON 2

OBJECTIVES
- To identify some Christmas vocabulary.
- To learn some family vocabulary.
- To recognise the importance of thinking about others, especially at Christmas.

LANGUAGE
Father, mother, brother, sister, baby.

RECEPTIVE LANGUAGE
Father Christmas, snowman, star, presents. Find (three)(mothers). Who's this?

REVISION
The numbers one to four

MATERIALS
Scissors. Personalised puppets. Photocopies of the Christmas card template (page 80 of the *Resource Bank*). Crayons.

Beginning the lesson

- Go through the family members on page 21 of the *Pupil's Book*. As you say each member of the family have the children repeat with you. Then say: *Open your books at page 27.* Hand out the scissors and have the children cut out the cards as outlined in previous units. Then go through each one saying: *Show me (the mother)!* The children hold up the corresponding card.

- Ask the children to get into groups of four. They should put their cards together on the table. Now say: *Find (three) (mothers).* The children group together their cards accordingly. Practise with the family members and the numbers one to four.

Developing the lesson

ACTIVITY 1
- Ask the children to open their *Pupil's Books* at pages 22 and 23. Give them a few minutes to look at the pages and then ask them what they can see (Banana at home, by the fire). Ask the children what they think Banana is doing, and why (writing Christmas cards for his family because it's Christmas). Point out the importance of thinking about others, especially at Christmas, to the children. Show the children the family members in the left-hand column, and ask: *Who's this?*, eliciting the different family members.

ACTIVITY 2
- Now show the children the items in the right-hand column and ask them what they can see. As they name each Christmas object or person say: *Yes, a star / Father Christmas / a snowman / Christmas presents.* Give the children a few minutes to find these objects in the main pictures. Hand out the personalised puppets and tell the children they are going to listen to Banana thinking about who he is going to send the different cards to. As they listen they should point to the corresponding picture with their personalised puppet. Stop after each of Banana's comments to give the children time to find the corresponding picture. (You may wish to play each section twice.)

R·15

picture 1
Banana:
Hmmm! A star for my mother and father. Happy Christmas!

picture 2
Hmmm! Father Christmas for the baby. Happy Christmas!

picture 3
Hmmm! A snowman for my brother. Happy Christmas, brother!

picture 4
And Christmas presents for my sister. Happy Christmas sister! Happy Christmas everybody!

Ending the lesson

- Draw the four Christmas items (Father Christmas, the snowman, the presents and the star) on the board, each with a square around to represent a Christmas card. Say the names of the family members and have the children point to the corresponding card that they will receive. Encourage the children to say the word in English.

- **EVALUATION:** Hand out the photocopies of the Christmas card template and explain to the children that they are going to make Christmas cards for their families. Show the children how to fold the paper to make a card, and then ask them to draw in the space the family member(s) they wish to give the card to. As the children work, go round asking: *Who's this?* Hand out crayons for the children to colour their cards. (You may wish the children to write inside *For mother / father*, etc.)

Reinforcement activity

- Play *Snap!* The children work in groups of four and put their cards together in the middle of the table in a pile. Each child takes it in turn to turn over a card, and place it on the 'turned over' pile at the side. If the card is the same as the previous card turned over, the child needs to say *Snap!* and name the family member to be able to keep the pair. The child with the most pairs wins the game.

Extension activity

- Repeat the reinforcement activity. The children play the game in the same way, but when the two cards coincide, it is the quickest child in the group to say *Snap!* who then has the possibility of naming the family member to be able to keep the cards.

Workbook   Page 16

- Say: *Open your workbooks at page16.* The activity revises the parts of the body that the children have learnt. Go through each row and describe what one of the family members is doing (touching his / her eye, etc.). The children should circle the corresponding family member. Do an example on the board.

UNIT 3

My family

OBJECTIVES
- To learn some Christmas vocabulary.
- To learn the numbers *five* and *six*.
- To reinforce the importance of thinking about others at Christmas.

LANGUAGE
Father Christmas, snowman, star, presents, five, six.

RECEPTIVE LANGUAGE
Which is your favourite?

REVISION
The colours learnt so far.

MATERIALS
A set of family cutout cards. Scissors. Glue. Coloured crayons: green, yellow, red, blue, orange, brown. Photocopies of the Christmas present template (page 81 of the *Resource Bank*).

Beginning the lesson

- Play the *Disappearing Game*. Stick a set of family cutout cards on the board and elicit all the family names from the children. Say: *Who's this?* as you point to each one. Then instruct a child to come and remove one of the family members. The children should then tell you all the family members, although one is missing. Repeat until all the cards have been removed from the board, but the children are able to tell you all the names.

Developing the lesson

ACTIVITY 1
- Say: *Open your books at page 23.* Take the children to the column on the right of the page and elicit the new language from the children asking: *What's this? (Father Christmas, snowman, star, presents).*
- Now ask the children: *Which is your favourite?* Go through the four Christmas objects and characters and ask the children to put up their hands when you reach their favourite.
- Tell the children that they are going to make a Christmas present for a member of their family. They should first decide who they are going to give it to, and what they want to give. Hand out the photocopies of the Christmas present template, along with the scissors and the glue. The children should first draw their present in the box, and then cut the sheet in two. They cut along the dotted line and then stick the "wrapping paper" on the present. Finally the children complete the tag for the present, either with the name of the person they want to give it to, or by drawing a picture. When the children have finished, have them show and describe their presents to each other. Again, reiterate that Christmas is a time for thinking about others.

ACTIVITY 2
- Write the numbers one to four on the board and have the children count with you. Then add the number five, say: *Look, five!* Have the children repeat *five* after you. Continue for the number *six*. Now show the children your two fists and slowly reveal a finger at a time, counting from one to six as you do so. Repeat, and encourage the children to do the same.
- Hand out the coloured crayons. Take the children back to pages 22 and 23 in their *Pupil's Books* and say: *Find the number one! Colour number one (blue)!* Repeat for the rest of the numbers and colours. Now name one of the colours, the children should tell you the corresponding number. Continue for all the colours and numbers.

Ending the lesson

- 🎧 Play the *Goodbye* chant (R – 2). Say: *Arms up! Hold hands!* The children join hands and chant along.

Reinforcement activity
- The children will need their family cutout cards for this activity. Give the children instructions to show you two members of Banana's family together. Say: *Show me the (mother) and the (baby), etc.*

Extension activity
- The children repeat the counting activity with their fingers, but now make their fingers disappear, and count down from six to one.

Workbook
Page **17**
- Say: *Open your workbooks at page 17.* Ask the children what and who they can see on the page (Christmas cards and Father Christmas). Tell the children to listen carefully to your instructions, as you are going to tell them what they should draw on the cards. Say: *Card number two, draw a star. Card number three, draw a present. Card number four, draw a snowman.* The children then colour their pictures. Ask them to think of family and friends they wish to give the cards to. As the children work go round asking them who the cards are for.

38

TEACHING NOTES

OBJECTIVES
- To learn the unit song.
- To revise the numbers one to six.

LANGUAGE
Christmas tree, bell.

REVISION
The numbers one to six. *How many (presents)?*

MATERIAL
Happy Christmas! poster. Photocopies of the snowman lantern template (page 82 of the *Resource Bank*). Scissors, crayons and glue.

Beginning the lesson

- Put up the *Happy Christmas! poster* and have the children study it carefully. Ask them what the different family members are holding. Then take the poster down. Challenge them to draw the four Christmas cards and say what they are.

- Draw the silhouette of a Christmas tree on the board and ask the children what it is. Say: *Yes, it's a Christmas tree.* Ask the children if they have one in their homes at Christmas, when they put it up, what they use to decorate it, etc. Tell the children that in today's lesson they are going to learn a song about a Christmas tree.

Developing the lesson

ACTIVITY 1
- Have the children open their *Pupil's Books* at page 24. Say: *Look! A Christmas tree!* Continue with: *Look! Snowmen! Look! Presents!* Continue with the other objects, teaching the new word *bell.* Then ask: *How many snowmen?* Draw a snowman on the board and have the children count the number of snowmen on the tree. Write the number next to the drawing on the board (6). Do the same for the presents (5), the Father Christmases (4), the bells (3), the stars (2), and finally the tree itself (1).

ACTIVITY 2
Now play the Christmas song. First let the children listen, point to the objects on the board as they 'appear' in the song, along with their corresponding number.

R•16 🎧

Look at the tree, The Christmas tree. With two bright stars, Yes, two bright stars on the Christmas tree.	Yes, two bright stars on the Christmas tree.
Look at the tree, The Christmas tree. With three happy bells, And two bright stars,	Look at the tree, The Christmas tree. With four Father Christmases, Three happy bells, And two bright stars, Yes, two bright stars on the Christmas tree.

Look at the tree, the Christmas tree.
With five Christmas presents,
Four Father Christmases,
Three happy bells,
And two bright stars,
Yes, two bright stars on the Christmas tree.

Look at the tree, the Christmas tree.
With six white snowmen,
Five Christmas presents,
Four Father Christmases,
Three happy bells,
And two bright stars,
Yes, two bright stars on one Christmas tree.

Ending the lesson

- Play the song again and encourage the children to join in. They should point to the different objects on the tree as they listen.

- **EVALUATION:** Take the children to the numbers at the bottom of the page and have them trace and complete them. As the children are working, go round and ask: *What number is this?* Finally the children colour the Christmas tree in the colours of their choice. Use this as an opportunity to evaluate the progress of several children.

Reinforcement activity

- Draw the silhouette of the Christmas tree on the board again and ask individual children to come and draw the decorations. Say: *Draw a star / bell / Father Christmas / present / snowman.*

Extension activity

- Hand out the photocopies of the snowman lantern along with scissors, crayons and glue. First the children colour their lanterns. Then show them how to cut the lanterns out and make the handle. The children can take the lanterns home to decorate their Christmas tree.

 **Workbook**   Page **18**

- Say: *Open your workbooks at page 18.* Ask the children who they can see at the top of the page (Banana's family). The children should follow the paths to see which decoration each member of the family is going to hang on the Christmas tree. The children then draw the decorations on the tree at the end of the paths. (Father - the star; mother - the bell; brother - the snowman; sister - the present; baby - the Father Christmas.)

My family

OBJECTIVES

- To practise vocabulary related to the family and Christmas.
- To enjoy listening to a story in English.
- To recognise the importance of wearing the appropriate clothes according to the weather.

RECEPTIVE LANGUAGE

Banana skin. Oh no! Oh dear! My arms! My legs! My hands!

MATERIALS

Family cutout cards. Dice for the *Workbook* activity.

Beginning the lesson

- Play *Musical cards*. Have a set of the family cutout cards ready. Hand out the cards and play some lively music, the children pass round the cards in time to the music. When you stop the music, the children with the cards stand up and say the name of the family member that they are holding.

Developing the lesson

- Tell the children it's time for a story, and have them come and sit round you in a semi-circle if possible. Show granny at the top of page 25 of the *Pupil's Book*, and explain that they are going to listen to a story about Banana and his family at Christmas. First ask the children to tell you what the weather is like at Christmas, and what kind of things they wear when they go out (coats, scarves, gloves, hats, etc.)

- Show the children the first scene. Say: *Look! Who is it?* Elicit: *Father, mother, sister, brother, baby* and *Banana*. Ask the children what is happening (the family are walking home through the snow, but it's very slippy because of the snow). Now ask the children what they think is going to happen next. (Is someone going to fall?)

- Tell the story, pause after each picture and invite the children to predict what will happen next. For each picture ask who they think is going to fall next, and why.

R•17

The banana skin

picture 1
Father: Whoooa! Careful everybody! Careful!
Baby: I'm happy! I'm happy in the snow, with my mother, and my father, and my sister and my brother! And Banana. This is fun, hee hee hee!

picture 2
Brother: Whoooa! Oh no! Owww! My legs!
Mother: Oh dear! Oh dear!

picture 3
Sister: Ooohh! Oh no! Ouch! My arms!
Mother and father: Oh dear! Oh dear, oh dear!

picture 4
Baby: Ooooh! Oh no! Waah waah! Waah! Waah! My hands! My hands! Waah! Waah!
Mother and father, Banana and the brother and sister:
Oh dear! Oh dear, oh dear, oh dear!

picture 5
Father: Here we are. Home at last. Come on everybody, inside. Inside everybody, Mother, brother, sister, Banana and baby, and m ... Whooooa!
Mother: Oh dear!

- Ask the children why the father has fallen (because of the banana skin!), and what they think the family does next. Explain that the family goes to the hospital because the father has broken his leg, and the result is the plaster cast on the father's leg - which they saw at the beginning of the unit (show the cutout card of the father again). Point out to the children the importance of being dressed in suitable clothes and shoes according to the weather.

- Ask the children to take their family cutout cards and to place them on their desks. Play the recorded story for the children, pausing after each scene. As the children listen they should order their cards according to the different members of the family falling over. Finally go over the order with the children.

Ending the lesson

- Play the *End of the story* song, which follows the story recording, and encourage the children to sing along.

Reinforcement activity

- Act out the story with the children. Divide the class into groups of six and allocate the family roles to the children. The children should hold hands forming a line. Retell the story to the children, who mime the actions. They mime falling in the snow, the other children try to stop them from falling over.

Extension activity

- Make a class graph to represent the number of brothers and sisters the children have. First start with the brothers. Get the children into groups according to the number of brothers they have. Count the children in each group and make a note of the number. Do the same for sisters, and then finally ask the children to put up their hand if there is a baby in their family. Count the hands. Prepare a bar graph with the results and have the children help you colour it to display it on the wall.

orkbook   Page **19**

- Hand out the dice and say: *Open your workbooks at page 19. Pair up the children. They take it in turns to throw the dice and draw the corresponding decorations on the Christmas tree in their own book.*

My family

OBJECTIVES
- To revise and consolidate the key language from the unit.
- To provide an opportunity for the children to reflect on the things they have done in this unit.

MATERIALS
Happy Christmas! poster. Family cutout cards. Photocopies of *Revision Sheet for Unit 3* (see *Evaluation* page 100). Crayons.

Beginning the lesson

- Put up the *poster*. Now give instructions to individual children to come to the front and indicate different objects on the poster. Say: *Point to the (Christmas tree).* You may alternatively have the children draw different Christmas decorations for the tree and come and stick them on the tree, saying what the decoration is at the same time.

- Ask individual children questions about the poster. Point to the family members and say: *Who's this?* Point to the different objects and say: *What's this?* Then ask about the colours: *What colour is (this present)?,* and ask: *How many (stars) are there?*

- Make sure the children have their family cutout cards. Get the children into groups of three, ask them to group together their cards and then play the card game 5 as described on page 77 of the *Resource Bank*.

Developing the lesson

- Take the children to **My English dictionary** on page 26. Play the recording of the vocabulary, the children listen and point in their books. Then go through the pictures again and elicit the language from the children.

R•18 🎧

- Father, mother, sister, brother, baby.
- Look! Stars! One, two, three, four, five, six stars.
- Father Christmas; snowman; presents; Christmas tree.

- **SELF-EVALUATION:** Tell the children they have worked well in this unit and show them their gold stars. Say: *Take a star and stick it here,* pointing to the end of Banana's magic wand on page 26. Then play the *Yaka Boo!* chant, encouraging the children to join in.

Ending the lesson

- Hand out the children's envelopes so they can store their cutout cards. Encourage the children to clip each set together with a paper clip to help keep them organised.

END OF UNIT EVALUATION

- Hand out the photocopies of the *Revision Sheet for Unit 3*, which can be found on page 100. The indications on how to carry out the evaluation are outlined on page 95.

Workbook   Page 20

- Say: *Open your workbooks at page 20.* Hand out the crayons. The children draw themselves with their family, or with their family and friends, at Christmas, in the Christmas frame.

My house

LESSON 1

OBJECTIVES
• To identify rooms of the house.
• To learn the unit chant.

LANGUAGE
House, bedroom, bathroom, living room, kitchen.

RECEPTIVE LANGUAGE
Come with me. Let's go to Banana's house! My (mother) is in the (living room). Point to the (living room). (Red) bedrooms can go!

REVISION
Parts of the body. Members of the family. Colours.

MATERIALS
Banana and Chocolate *flashcards*. Personalised puppets.

Beginning the lesson

• Allocate roles to the class of *brother* (for the boys), and *sister* (for the girls). Check the children are clear about their roles. Say: *Hands up, brothers,* etc. Now play *Touch Your ...* Say: *Touch your (nose), (sisters)! Touch your (feet), (brothers)!* Continue with the different parts of the body that they have learnt in unit 2 *(hands, arms, legs, eyes, mouth).*

Developing the lesson

• Using the Chocolate *flashcard* say: *Hello, everybody!* and encourage the children to reply: *Hello, Chocolate.* Through Chocolate tell the children you are going to visit Banana's house, and that it is a very special house. Show the children how to use their fingers to indicate walking, and say: *Come with me. Let's go to Banana's house!*

• Say: *Open your books at page 29.* Take the Banana *flashcard* and say: *Look, this is my house!* In L1 ask the children what is special about the house (it's under the sea!) and ask them a little about what they can see in the picture (an octopus, fish, etc.) Now hand out the children's personalised puppets and have them follow Banana's instructions: *My mother is in the living room. Point to the living room.* The children listen and point to the corresponding room. Repeat with the different members of the family and the different rooms, giving the children time to listen and point. Finally ask the children to find Chocolate in the house (he's in the lift, on his way to Banana's bedroom).

• Tell the children they are going to learn a chant about the house, sung by the octopus. First let the children listen and point to the different rooms with their puppets. Then play the chant again and teach them the actions. The children chant along and do the actions.

R·19 🎧

I am an octopus, /stretch fingers in and out like tentacles/
One, two, three. /count to three on fingers/
I am an octopus, /stretch fingers in and out/
Under the sea. /make wave actions/

This is a house, /put hands above head to make a roof/
One, two, three.
This is a house,
Under the sea.

This is the living room, /read an imaginary book with your hands/
One, two, three.
This is the living room,
Under the sea.

This is the kitchen, /stir an imaginary pot as if cooking/

One, two, three.
This is the kitchen,
Under the sea.

This is the bathroom, /wash your face with your hands/
One, two, three.
This is the bathroom,
Under the sea.

This is the bedroom, /put two hands on one side of your head to indicate sleeping/
One, two, three.
This is the bedroom,
Under the sea.

I am an octopus,
One, two, three.
I am an octopus,
Under ... the ... SEA!

Ending the lesson

• Ask the children to think of their favourite colour for a bedroom. Go through the colours the children have learnt and ask them to put up their hands if they have chosen that colour. Then have the children leave by saying: *(Red) bedrooms can go!* Repeat until you have gone through all the colours.

Reinforcement activity

• Draw a house on the board and ask: *What's this?* Then draw in the kitchen, the living room, the bedroom and the bathroom, stopping after each to ask: *What's this?* When the house is complete invite individual children to come to the front and remove the rooms. Say: *Rub out the living room,* etc.

Extension activity

• Go round the class asking individual children: *What colour is your bedroom?* The children then work in pairs and ask each other using their puppets.

orkbook
Page **21**

• Say: *Open your workbooks at page 21.* The children first match the characters with their corresponding homes, and then colour in the pictures. Go over the activity with the whole class.

TEACHING NOTES

My house

LESSON 2

OBJECTIVES
- To learn some furniture vocabulary.
- To relate items of furniture to their corresponding rooms.

LANGUAGE
Bed, fridge, bath, sofa.

RECEPTIVE LANGUAGE
Number (threes), go to the (bathroom). Look! A (bath). Which room? Where's the (fridge)? In the (kitchen). Sofas can go!

REVISION
Rooms of the house.

MATERIALS
A set of cutout cards from page 35 of the *Pupil's Book*. Photocopies of the house template (page 83 of the *Resource Bank*). Scissors, glue and crayons.

Beginning the lesson

- Draw a house on the board and elicit the names of the four rooms from the previous lesson. Using the 'room' cutout cards, give each corner of the classroom the name of a room and place the card there. Divide the class into four groups and number them from one to four. Now give the following instructions, say: *Number (threes), go to the (bathroom).* The children move to the corresponding room. Repeat the instructions changing the rooms so that the children move round the classroom, visiting the different rooms of the house.

Developing the lesson

- The children should stay in the 'rooms'. Take the furniture cutout cards (the sofa, the fridge, the bath and the bed). Hold them up one at a time and say: *Look! A (bath). Which room?* The children in the 'bathroom' should indicate their room. Hand over the corresponding card. Repeat for the four items of furniture.

- Have the children sit down and ask them to open their *Pupil's Books* at pages 30 and 31. Give the children a few minutes to have a good look at the page. Then take them to the column on the left of page 30 and say: *Point to the bed, point to the fridge,* etc. Repeat, changing the order of the items of furniture. Now ask the children to find the furniture in the main picture.

- Tell the children they are going to listen to someone asking about where the different pieces of furniture are. They should listen carefully and find the room. Play the recording, stopping after each question to give the children time to find it in the main picture. Then encourage them to respond, before playing the recorded answer.

R•20

1 Where's the fridge? In the kitchen.	**3** Where's the bath? In the bathroom.
2 Where's the bed? In the bedroom.	**4** Where's the sofa? In the living room.

Ending the lesson

- Ask the children to decide which piece of furniture they want to be (from the four items they have learnt). When they are ready have the children leave by saying: *Sofas can go!,* etc. With stronger groups you can also ask them to think of the colour, and dismiss the class according to colour and item of furniture: *(Red sofas) can go!.*

Reinforcement activity

- Name one of the items of furniture, say: *Sofa!,* the children reply: *Living room.* Then reverse roles, say: *Kitchen!* The children reply: *Fridge.* Repeat for the other rooms and furniture.

Extension activity

- Hand out the photocopies of the house template, the scissors, glue and crayons. The children should first draw furniture in the two rooms of the house (as seen through the window). They decide which rooms they are and draw the corresponding furniture. Show the children how to cut and separate the two parts of the sheet, as well as how to cut around the shutters. They stick the front part of the house over the part they have illustrated. When the children are ready, divide the class into groups of four, they show the other children in their groups the houses, opening the shutters and naming the rooms and the furniture inside. The houses can also be used to play a guessing game. The children try to guess which room is behind the shutters.

Workbook   Page 22

- Say: *Open your workbooks at page 22.* Hand out coloured crayons and give the children the following indications for the colour patches. Say: *Colour number one blue. Colour number two orange. Colour number three red. Colour number four green. Colour number five yellow. Colour number six brown.* The children then colour the house picture following the number code.

My house

OBJECTIVES
- To identify different household activities.
- To recognise the importance of helping out in the house.

RECEPTIVE LANGUAGE
Who's this? Where's the (father)? Find the (father). Who's in the bedroom? Yes, he/she's playing / washing up / reading / brushing her teeth.

REVISION
Members of the family. The numbers one to four.

MATERIALS
Chocolate *flashcard*. Scissors. Cutout card envelopes.

Beginning the lesson

- Play *'Chocolate Says'* with the following instructions: *Stand up! Be big! Be small! Run! Be happy! Be sad! Jump! Sit down!*

Developing the lesson

ACTIVITY 1
- Say: *Open your books at page 31.* Point to the column on the right of page 31 and ask: *Who's this?* for each of the characters *(father, mother, brother, sister)*. Now say: *Where's the father? Find the father.* Elicit: *In the kitchen.* Go through each of the members of the family, giving the children time to find them in the main picture. Then change over and ask about the rooms. Say: *Who's in the bedroom?*, etc.

- Now ask the children to look closely and to tell you (in L1) what each member of the family is doing. (The father is washing up, the mother is brushing her teeth, the brother is playing and the sister is reading.) As they tell you, say: *Yes, (he) is (playing).* Go through the family members and the different activities, teaching the children the actions for them. Finally say the family member names at random, the children should listen and mime the corresponding actions.

ACTIVITY 2
- **EVALUATION:** Hand out the scissors and take the children to the cutout cards on page 35 of their *Pupil's Books*. Have the children cut out the cards following the procedure outlined in previous units. Go through the vocabulary, the children listen and hold up the corresponding card. The children then work in pairs with one set of cards and play *The Memory Game*. They should place the cards face down on the desk and take it in turns to find two matching cards (the item of furniture and the room). On finding matching cards the child needs to name both to be able to 'win' the pair. The game continues until all the cards have been won. As they work, go round the class evaluating the progress of several children.

Ending the lesson

- Finally go through the cards of the different rooms and in L1 ask the children what Banana and Chocolate are doing. When you come to the kitchen, with Banana and Chocolate washing up, ask the children if they help out at home and what kinds of things they do. Emphasise the importance of everyone helping out in the house and sharing the work. Finally hand out the cutout card envelopes and have the children put their cards away.

Reinforcement activity

- The children work with the cutout cards. Name a room, the children should hold up and name the corresponding item of furniture. Then change over, name the furniture, the children hold up and name the corresponding room.

Extension activity

- Do a drawing dictation. Ask the children to draw a house with a bedroom, a bathroom, a kitchen and a living room. Then give the following instructions:

  The father is in the living room.
  The mother is in the bedroom.
  The brother is in the bathroom.
  The sister is in the kitchen.
  There are three chairs in the kitchen.
  There are two beds in the bedroom.
  There is a cat in the living room.
  There are four books in the bedroom.

 **Workbook**   Page **23**

- Say: *Open your workbooks at page 23.* The children join the dots to form the three items of furniture. Go over them with the children (fridge, bed, sofa). They can then colour the furniture.

OBJECTIVES
- To identify rooms according to their respective sounds.
- To enjoy practising the new language from the unit in a game.

LANGUAGE
Where's Banana / Chocolate? In the (bathroom).

REVISION
The rooms of the house.

MATERIALS
Stickers for this lesson. Sheets of paper and crayons.

Beginning the lesson

- Say the names of the different rooms in the house. The children should mime the corresponding activities from the previous lesson. When the children are comfortable with the actions, play *Race the Teacher,* and see if they can do the actions before you.

Developing the lesson

ACTIVITY 1
- Say: *Open your books at page 32.* Give the children a moment to look at the page and then ask: *Where's Banana?* Go through each number, and elicit from the children the names of the rooms of the house (according to where Banana is).

- Show the children the stickers which correspond to this page. Now explain to the children that they are going to listen and try to identify exactly where Banana is. They will hear some sounds of Banana in that room. They should take one of the 'tick' stickers and stick it on the corresponding picture. Play the recording, stopping after each sound. Give the children time to take the sticker and stick it in the corresponding place.

R•21

1. /sounds of pans clattering in the kitchen/
2. /sounds of Banana in the shower singing/
3. /sounds of the television in the living room/
4. /sounds of Banana snoring in bed in the bedroom/

ACTIVITY 2
- **EVALUATION:** Go over each room with the children, asking: *Where's Banana?* and eliciting the answers. Now hand out small pieces of paper about 30mm square and ask the children to draw either Banana or Chocolate on the paper. Then say: *Open your books at pages 30 and 31.* Tell the children they should hide either Chocolate or Banana (depending on who they have drawn) in one of the rooms of the house (being careful not to let anyone see). The children then play in pairs and try to find where Chocolate / Banana is hiding. The first child asks: *Where's (Banana)?* The second child should then

guess, saying: *In the (bathroom),* etc. When the child guesses correctly they change roles. As the children play, go round the class and check on the development of several children.

Ending the lesson

- End the lesson with the *Goodbye* chant (R – 2).

Reinforcement activity

- Hand out sheets of paper and crayons. Tell the children they are going to draw a picture of Chocolate's house, and Chocolate's family in the house doing different things. As the children work, go round asking: *Who's this?,* and *What is he / she doing?*

Extension activity

- Hand out more small paper squares. Play the game from *Developing the lesson.* This time the children should draw any of the Halloween characters from unit 2 that they have learnt (the witch, the monster, the ghost, the skeleton, the cat) and hide them in one of the rooms in the house. The first child begins with: *Where's the (ghost)?*

My house

LESSON 5

OBJECTIVES
- To practise vocabulary related to the house.
- To enjoy listening to a story in English.
- To learn about a traditional English children's game.

RECEPTIVE LANGUAGE
Not in the (kitchen). Under the bed!

REVISION
The numbers one to six. Rooms of the house.

MATERIALS
A set of cutout cards. Four bed sheets to act out the story. Two small squares of paper.

Beginning the lesson

- Draw Banana and Chocolate on the underside of two small squares of paper and place them in different rooms in the house on pages 30 and 31. Put one or two other squares of paper in the other rooms. Show the children the pages and ask: *Where's (Banana)?* As they tell you the names of the rooms, look at the corresponding square of paper. If the picture corresponds show the children and say: *Well done.* If not, put the paper square back and continue the game. Alternatively you may wish to hide the Halloween characters from unit 2.

Developing the lesson

- Tell the children that it's time for a story, and have them come and sit round you in a semi-circle if possible. Show granny at the top of page 33 of the *Pupil's Book*, and explain that they are going to listen to a story about Banana and Chocolate playing a game called *Hide and Seek* in the house. Point to the first picture of the story and ask them what is happening (Chocolate has got his eyes covered and is counting, whilst Banana runs away to hide). Ask the children what they think will happen next.

- Tell the story, pause after each picture and invite the children to guess where Chocolate is going to look next.

R•22

Hide and seek

picture 1
Banana: Hee! Hee! Hee!
Chocolate:
One, two, three, four, five, six!
Ready! Where are you?

picture 2
Chocolate:
Where are you, Banana?
Hmmm! Not in the kitchen.

picture 3
Chocolate:
Hmmm! Not in the bathroom.

picture 4
Chocolate:
Hmmm! Not in the living room.

picture 5
Chocolate:
And not in the ... Yes!!! In the bedroom!!!
Banana:
Oh no!
Chocolate:
Banana is IN the bedroom, UNDER the bed!
Banana and Chocolate:
Ha ha ha ha ha!

- Ask: *Where is Banana?*, eliciting: *In the bedroom.* Then say: *Yes, in the bedroom and under the bed,* pointing to Banana under the bed as you do so. Ask the children if they have ever played this game and where they normally play it. Now play the recording of the story and let the children follow in their books.

Ending the lesson

- Play the *End of the story* song, and encourage the children to sing along.

Reinforcement activity

- Retell the story but this time change the order of the rooms where Chocolate looks. The children should listen carefully and follow in their books. When they hear a different room they should shout out: *No!*, and correct you.

Extension activity

- Act out the story with the class. Using the room cutout cards, allocate rooms of the house to the four corners of the classroom and go over them with the whole class until they are clear which 'room' is which. Have two children play the parts of Banana and Chocolate, and three children to play the parts of 'jokers'. Chocolate should cover his eyes whilst Banana and the other three children hide in the 'rooms' of the house (they should crouch down, and be covered with a sheet). When the children are well hidden, the rest of the class should count to six with Chocolate and then shout: *Ready!* Chocolate goes from 'room' to 'room' looking for Banana. As each sheet is removed, the class shouts: *Not in the (kitchen),* or *Yes, in the (bathroom).* Repeat with different children playing the parts of Banana, Chocolate and the other three children.

W orkbook   Page **24**

- Say: *Open your workbooks at page 24.* The children should order the pictures according to the original story. Go over the order with the children.

- **OBJECTIVES**
  - To revise and consolidate the key language from the unit.
  - To recognise the importance of brushing one's teeth after meals.
  - To provide an opportunity for the children to reflect on the things they have done in this unit.

- **MATERIALS**

  A set of cutout cards. Star stickers, one per child. Photocopies of the *Revision Sheet for Unit 4* (see *Evaluation* page 101).

Beginning the lesson

- Begin the lesson with the following miming game. The children listen and follow your instructions. Say: *You are in the kitchen. You are washing the plates,* the children mime accordingly. Continue with: *You are in the living room, you are reading. You are in the bathroom, you are brushing your teeth. You are in the bedroom, you are playing.*

Developing the lesson

ACTIVITY 1

- Have the children take out the cutout room cards from their envelopes. Tell the children that they are going to hear a story about Banana and Chocolate, as they listen they should put the cards in the corresponding order. Tell the story as follows:

  Banana and Chocolate are in the house. They decide to wash the plates, so they go to the kitchen. They decide to brush their teeth so they go to the bathroom. Then they decide to play, so they go to the bedroom. And finally they decide to read so they go to the living room.

- Check the order with the children. Ask the children when they normally brush their teeth, and see if anyone knows why. Stress the importance of brushing your teeth after meals, just as Banana and Chocolate are doing in the card. Now play card game 6 on page 77 of the *Resource Bank*.

ACTIVITY 2

- Take the children to **My English dictionary** on page 34. Play the recording of the vocabulary, the children listen and point in their books. Then go through the pictures again and elicit the language from the children.

R•23 🎧

- Bedroom, living room, kitchen, bathroom.
- Bed, sofa, fridge, bath.
- House.

- **SELF-EVALUATION:** Tell the children they have worked well in this unit and show them their gold stars. Say: *Take a star and stick it here,* pointing to the end of Banana's magic wand on page 34. Then play the *Yaka Boo!* chant and encourage the children to join in.

Ending the lesson

- Hand out the children's envelopes so they can store their cards. Encourage the children to clip each set together with a paper clip to help keep them organised.

END OF UNIT EVALUATION

- Hand out the photocopies of the *Revision Sheet for Unit 4*, which can be found on page 101. The indications on how to carry out the evaluation are outlined on page 95.

Workbook   Page 25

- Hand out scissors and crayons and ask the children to open their *Workbooks* at page 25. Explain that they are going to make a notice for their bedroom door. They should first colour in the picture, and then complete their name at the bottom. Finally show them how to cut out the notice, taking care with the handle. The children can take the notice home to hang on the door handle of their bedroom.

My clothes

LESSON 1

OBJECTIVES
- To learn some clothes vocabulary.
- To learn the unit chant.

LANGUAGE
T-shirt, shorts, jumper, hat.

RECEPTIVE LANGUAGE
Draw an old (chair). Look! A mouse. If you're wearing a (jumper) you can go. Jump on the table. Run to the door.

REVISION
Furniture vocabulary from unit 4.

MATERIALS
A large old T-shirt, hat, jumper and some shorts. *Flashcards:* hat, T-shirt, jumper, shorts. An envelope large enough for the *flashcards.*

Beginning the lesson

- Draw an old house on the board with a very big attic. In L1 ask the children about this part of a house and what you might find there. Now invite the children to come to the board and draw items of furniture that they have learnt. Say: *Draw an old chair. Draw an old sofa.* Encourage the children to draw things which are old. Now draw a table yourself, and say: *Look! An old table.* Continue and draw a mouse next to the table. Say: *And look! A mouse.*

Developing the lesson

ACTIVITY 1

- Tell the children that Banana and Chocolate are in an attic, and ask them to open their *Pupil's Books* at page 37.

- Give the children a few minutes to look at the page and then ask them what Banana and Chocolate are doing (they are standing on the table), and why (they are frightened of the mouse). Tell the children they are going to listen to a chant about Banana and Chocolate, but first they are going to learn the actions. Show the children how to mime jumping onto the table, and then how to mime running to the door. Play the chant, first let the children listen and do the actions, then have them mime the actions and chant along.

R•24 🎧

Look! A mouse!
Jump on the table!
Jump on the table!
Look! A mouse!
Run to the door!
Run to the door!
(repeat)

- Ask the children if they like mice, or if they are frightened of them like Banana and Chocolate. Ask the children to look carefully at page 37 and tell you anything else they can see (clothes). Explain that in this unit they are going to learn to talk about clothes in English. Ask them to close their books. Take the old hat, the T-shirt, the jumper and the shorts and invite children to come to the front and put them on. As they put on the clothes say the word and have the class repeat with you. Alternatively, use the *flashcards* to present the language.

ACTIVITY 2

- Now play *What is it?* Have the four clothes *flashcards* ready inside the envelope. Divide the class into two teams. Hold the envelope so that all the children can see. Slowly make one of the cards start to appear. Ask: *What is it? What is it?* As soon as someone shouts out the correct answer, their team wins the card.

Ending the lesson

- Have the children leave by saying: *If you're wearing a (jumper) you can go.* Use the four clothes items learnt in the lesson.

Reinforcement activity

- Play the chant again and have the children join in.

Extension activity

- Play *What is it?* but include *flashcards* of vocabulary that the children have learnt in previous units. Choose from parts of the body, Halloween characters and classroom objects.

Workbook   Page 27

- Say: *Open your workbooks at page 27.* Ask the children what they can see in the top picture (Chocolate looking frightened of the mouse). The children use the squares to reproduce the picture in the grid below. Emphasise the importance of looking closely at the squares and using them to help guide their drawings.

My clothes

OBJECTIVES

• To learn more clothes vocabulary.

LANGUAGE

Dress, shirt, trousers, shoes.

RECEPTIVE LANGUAGE

Who's wearing a (jumper)? Look! A (dress). Find the (dress).

REVISION

Clothes vocabulary from the previous lesson. Members of the family.

MATERIALS

The clothes from the previous lesson or the cutout clothes cards from page 43 of the *Pupil's Book. The Family Party poster.* Personalised puppets. Lively music.

Beginning the lesson

• Remind the children of the story from unit 3 about Banana and family walking home in the snow. See if they can remember the kinds of clothes they were wearing. Show the four items of clothing from the previous lesson or stick the four clothes *flashcards* on the board (T-shirt, hat, jumper and shorts). Ask the children which things they wear in the winter, in the snow, and which they wear in the summer.

Developing the lesson

• **EVALUATION:** Put up the *poster* and give the children a few moments to look at it. Ask them who they can see (Banana and Chocolate and family), and what they are doing (having a music party). Now ask: *Who's wearing a jumper?* (hold up the flashcard at the same time and point to the poster). Elicit: *The brother.* Ask: *Who's wearing a hat?* Elicit: *Banana.* Ask: *Who's wearing shorts?* Elicit: *The sister.* And finally: *Who's wearing a T-shirt?* Elicit: *The sister / Chocolate.* Use this opportunity to evaluate the progress of several children.

• Have the children open their *Pupil's Books* at pages 38 and 39. Hand out the personalised puppets and say: *Point to the hat, point to a T-shirt, point to the jumper, point to the shorts.* Then take the children to the column on the left of page 38 and say: *Look! A dress. Find the dress.* Help the children look for the dress in the main picture. Ask: *Who's wearing the dress?(The mother).* Point to the trousers in the column and say: *Look! Trousers. Find the trousers.* Then ask: *Who's wearing the trousers? (The father).* Do the same for the items in the left-hand column, introducing *shirt* and *shoes.*

Ending the lesson

• Now have the children leave saying: *If you're wearing a dress you can go!* Repeat with the new clothes vocabulary presented *(shirt, trousers)* and finally, *shoes.*

Reinforcement activity

• Have the children think of their favourite singer or star. Hand out sheets of paper and crayons, and tell the children that they are going to design an outfit for them. They should decide the colours and the items of clothes. As the children work go round asking: *What is it?* and *What colour is it?*

Extension activity

• Play *Musical cards* with a set of cutout clothes cards. Play some lively music, and have the children pass the cards around the class. When the music stops the children with the cards stand up and name the item of clothing on their card.

Workbook   Page **28**

• Say: *Open your workbooks at page 28.* The children do the clothes sums and write the answer in the boxes provided. Do the first sum with the whole class.

UNIT **5**

My clothes

LESSON 3

OBJECTIVES
• To learn the colours *purple* and *white*.

LANGUAGE
Purple, white.

RECEPTIVE LANGUAGE
What colour is the (shirt)?

REVISION
Colours learnt so far. Members of the family.

MATERIALS
The Family Party poster. Colour *flashcards*: yellow, red, blue, green, orange, brown, black, white, purple. Sheets of paper and crayons.

Beginning the lesson

• Stick the *flashcards* of the colours learnt so far across the board in the following order: red, brown, yellow, green, orange, black, blue. 'Chant' through them with the children.

• Put up the *poster*, point to the balloons and say: *Look! Balloons!* Then give individual children instructions to come and touch the different coloured balloons in the poster. Say: *Touch the (blue) balloon,* etc.

• Show the children the white *flashcard* and say: *White.* Have the children repeat with you, and then do the same for *purple*. Finally have children come and touch something *white* and *purple* in the poster.

Developing the lesson

• Add the white and purple *flashcards* to the 'list' of colours on the board. Now go through the clothes learnt in the previous two lessons on the *poster* (or the *Pupil's Book*, pages 38 and 39) and ask the children: *What colour is the (shirt)?*, pointing as you do to the father's shirt. Elicit: *White.* Go through different items of clothing in the *poster* and ask the children the colour.

• Tell the children they are going to listen to someone asking about the colours of the clothes in the poster. They should listen and try to answer. Stop after each question and point to the corresponding character on the poster, helping the children answer. Then play the answer on the recording.

R•25

What colour is the mother's dress?	What colour are Chocolate's shoes?
Purple.	Blue.
What colour are the father's trousers?	What colour are YOUR shoes?
Brown.	
What colour is the father's shirt?	
White.	

Ending the lesson

• End the lesson with the final question on the recording. Have the children look at their shoes and then tell their friend / the child sitting next to them the colour. Let the children leave the class according to their shoe colour. Say: *Brown shoes can go,* etc.

Reinforcement activity

• Hand out sheets of paper and crayons and have the children choose one of the family members from the poster. They should draw the family member. Form groups of four with the children, they take turns to show their drawings while the other members of the group try to guess who it is.

Extension activity

• Hand out sheets of paper and crayons. The children draw themselves in the clothes they are wearing today. As they work go round the class asking: *What's this?* and *What colour is it?*

NOTE: If you plan to use the Carnival costumes for the puppets in the reinforcement activity for the next lesson, you will need to ask the children which characters they want to be (witch, pirate, clown or magician). You will then need to prepare the photocopies for the costumes.

 **W**orkbook   Page **29**

• Say: *Open your workbooks at page 29.* The children follow Banana and Chocolate's paths, collecting the clothes along the way. When they get to the end they draw the corresponding clothes on Banana and Chocolate.

My clothes

 LESSON 4

OBJECTIVES
- To identify some Carnival vocabulary.
- To learn the unit song.

RECEPTIVE LANGUAGE
Magician, pirate. Stick the (black and white hat) on (Banana).

REVISION
Clothes vocabulary and colours.

MATERIALS
A set of cutout clothes cards. Stickers for this lesson. Photocopies of the puppet costume templates (pages 84 and 85 of the *Resource Bank*), depending on the characters chosen by the children in the previous lesson. Crayons, scissors. The personalised puppets. Two bags of large clothes, each containing: a dress, a shirt, shorts, trousers, shoes, a T-shirt, a jumper and a hat.

Beginning the lesson

- Show the children the stickers for this lesson and ask the children what Carnival costumes they think are represented (a pirate and a magician). Go through the stickers and see if the children can identify the items of clothing (hat, trousers and shirt – magician; hat, trousers and T-shirt – pirate). Then ask the children who they think the clothes are for (Banana and Chocolate).

Developing the lesson

- **EVALUATION:** Tell the children that Banana and Chocolate are getting ready for a Carnival party and that the children are going to help them. Say: *Open your Pupil's Books at page 40.* Make sure all the children have their stickers. Then say: *Stick the black hat on Banana. Stick the black trousers on Banana. Stick the white shirt on Banana.* Continue: *Stick the black hat on Chocolate, stick the blue trousers on Chocolate, stick the black and white T-shirt on Chocolate.* Go round helping the children stick on the stickers. Use this as an opportunity to evaluate the progress of several children.

- When the children are ready, play the song. Let the children listen and point in their books at Banana and Chocolate with their Carnival costumes on. Then play the song again and encourage the children to join in.

R•26 🎧

BANANA:	CHOCOLATE:
Hey everybody,	Hey everybody,
Look at me!	Look at me!
Look at me!	Look at me!
Look at me!	Look at me!
Black trousers,	Blue trousers,
White shirt,	Black and white T-shirt,
Black hat,	Black hat,
I'm a magician!	I'm a pirate!
Hey everybody,	Hey everybody,
Look at me!	Look at me!

Ending the lesson

- Divide the class into two groups, Banana and Chocolate. Play and sing the song again, this time the children sing their corresponding part.

Reinforcement activity

- Hand out the photocopies of the puppet costumes, the scissors, crayons and the children's personalised puppets. First the children should colour their costumes. Then help the children cut out the clothes and dress the personalised puppets. Show them how to fold the tabs over so that the clothes stay on. As the children work go round asking: *What are you?* Keep the puppets with the costumes for the Carnival party story in the next lesson.

Extension activity

- Play the *Dressing Up Game.* Divide the class into two teams, and give each team its set of clothes. A volunteer should come to the front from each team to be the 'dummy'. Now start the game. Take one of the cards at random and say the word, but don't show the picture. The team should select the correct item of clothing and go and dress the 'dummy'. When they are ready show the card and compare what they have chosen. If the clothing isn't correct the item should be returned. Continue until all the cards are finished. The team with most clothes on their 'dummy' is the winner.

🅦orkbook   Page **30**

- Say: *Open your workbooks at page 30.* First indicate to the children the colours they should use to colour the patches. Say: *Number one, blue. Number two, yellow. Number three, brown. Number four, green.* The children then colour Banana and Chocolate using this colour code. Finally the children count the number of bananas in the main picture and write the number in the square (there are six).

My clothes

OBJECTIVES
- To enjoy listening to a story in English.
- To learn a traditional English party game.

RECEPTIVE LANGUAGE
Clown. I'm Banana the magician. Boys and girls, quiet please! In the box please, Chocolate.

REVISION
Witch.

MATERIALS
Personalised puppets (in Carnival costume if used). A set of cutout clothes cards. A bar of chocolate, a knife (not sharp), a fork, a plate, one of the bags of clothes from the previous lesson, but with the hat, trousers, shoes and jumper only.

Beginning the lesson

- Tell the children that in today's lesson they are going to hear a story about Banana and Chocolate going to a Carnival party in their costumes. See if they can remember the costumes from the previous lesson. Ask the children if they dress up for Carnival, and if so, what was the last costume they wore.

- If the children have prepared their puppets with Carnival costumes hand them out so they too can go to the Carnival party.

Developing the lesson

- Have the children come and sit round you in a semi-circle (they should bring their puppets too). Show granny at the top of page 41 of the *Pupil's Book*, and ask the children if they are ready for the story.

- Point to the first picture and ask the children what they can see (Banana and Chocolate at the Carnival party. Banana is about to perform a magic trick, since he is a magician). Ask the children what other characters they can see (a witch and a clown). Say: *Yes, a witch and a clown*. Then ask them what they think is going to happen in the next picture (Banana is going to cut Chocolate into two?).

- Tell the story, pausing after each picture and inviting the children to predict what will happen next.

R•27

Banana's magic trick
picture 1
BANANA:
Boys and girls, quiet please! Quiet! I'm Banana the magician, and THIS is Chocolate.

BANANA:
In the box please, Chocolate.

picture 2
BANANA:

One Chocolate, and now, abracadabra ...
Two Chocolates!!!

picture 3
BANANA:
And now ...
Abracadabra ... Abracadabra ... Abracadabra ...

picture 4
BANANA:
Two small Chocolates!!!

- In L1 ask the children if Banana's trick is successful. See if they can remember the magic word (which was also used by the witch in unit 2): *Abracadabra*. Let the children listen again to the story, play the recording and let them follow in their books.

- Point out to the children Banana's use of the word *please*, and the importance of being polite when we ask someone to do something.

Ending the lesson

- Play the *End of the story* song and encourage the children to sing along.

- Play the following traditional party game. Have the bag of clothes ready and put the unwrapped bar of chocolate on a plate with the knife and fork at the side. The children take it in turns to play. You will need to time them, allowing two minutes per child. Show one of the clothes cards. The first child to say the item correctly has one minute to get dressed in that item of clothing and try to eat the chocolate with the knife and fork.

Reinforcement activity

- Revise the clothes vocabulary by holding up the cards one by one and have the children repeat the words after you. Say: *Close your eyes, everybody!* Hide a card from the pile. Show all the cards again and have the children repeat the words with you as you show them. The children raise their hands to tell you the missing card. The child who guesses correctly gets a turn at hiding a card.

Extension activity

- Ask the children if they have ever seen any magic tricks performed and have them describe them for the rest of the class.

Workbook   Page 31

- Say: *Open your workbooks at page 31*. The children match the characters on the left with their corresponding hats on the right by drawing a line, and then colour them. Do the first one with the children.

OBJECTIVES

- To revise and consolidate the key language from the unit.
- To provide an opportunity for the children to reflect on the things they have done in this unit.

MATERIALS

The Family Party poster. Scissors. Star stickers (one per child). Photocopies of the *Revision Sheet for Unit 5* (see *Evaluation* page 102).

Beginning the lesson

- Put up the *poster*. Give instructions, first working on the colours, say: *Find something (blue)*. The children go to the poster and point to something blue. Then repeat the procedure using clothes: *Find a (dress)*. Finally give descriptions of what the different family members are wearing: *He's wearing an orange jumper,* etc. The children should find the corresponding 'person'.

Developing the lesson

ACTIVITY 1

- Have the children turn to page 43 in their *Pupil's Books* and hand out the scissors. The children should cut out and prepare their cards as outlined in previous units. When the children are ready, play card game 7 on page 77 of the *Resource Bank*.

ACTIVITY 2

- Take the children to **My English dictionary** on page 42. Play the recording of the vocabulary, the children listen and point in their books. Then go through the pictures again and elicit the language from the children.

R•28

- Dress, T-shirt, trousers, jumper, hat, shorts, shoes, shirt.
- Look! The mouse is on the table!

- Tell the children they have worked well in this unit and show them their gold stars. Say: *Take a star and stick it here*, pointing to the end of Banana's magic wand on page 42. Then play the *Yaka Boo!* chant, encouraging the children to join in.

Ending the lesson

- Hand out the children's envelopes so they can store their cards. Remind the children to clip the set together with a paper clip to help keep them organised.

END OF UNIT EVALUATION

- Hand out the photocopies of the *Revision Sheet for Unit 5*, which can be found on page 102. The indications on how to carry out the evaluation are outlined on page 96.

Workbook   Page 32

- Say: *Open your workbooks at page 32*. The children should decide the costume they want to wear for Carnival and then draw their costume inside the Carnival frame. They then colour them. As the children work go round asking them about their costumes.

UNIT 6

Farm animals

OBJECTIVES
- To learn the names of some farm and domestic animals.
- To learn the unit song.

LANGUAGE
Cow, horse, pig, dog.

RECEPTIVE LANGUAGE
What can you see / hear? What's this? (Chocolate's) got a (dog). What's (Chocolate) got?

REVISION
Clothes vocabulary from unit 5. *Cat.*

MATERIALS
A set of clothes cutout cards from unit 5. Photocopies of page 86 of the *Resource Bank*. Crayons.

Beginning the lesson

- Revise the clothes vocabulary from unit 5 with a set of the cutout cards. Stick the cards across the board and go through each one saying: *Look! It's a (dress),* making some mistakes. Invite the children to say: *Yes* or *No* and to correct you. Now have the children watch you as you mime putting on one of the items of clothing. The children shout out what it is as soon as they identify it. Then have the children mime putting on the clothes for each other. You may wish to do this as a team game.

Developing the lesson

ACTIVITY 1
- Tell the children that Banana and Chocolate have just been to visit a farm, where they have learnt about different farm animals. Ask if they can tell you what kinds of animals live on a farm. Ask if any of them have been to a farm, and which animals were there. Invite the children to either make the noises of the different animals or to come and draw them on the board.
- Now say: *Open your books at page 45. What can you see?* Give the children a moment to look at the page and then ask them to find Banana and Chocolate. Ask them what they are doing (listening to the farmer, who is showing them some of the animals). Identify the animals on the page which correspond with the animals already mentioned. Then say: *Look! A cow! What can you hear?* Point to the cow on the page and invite the children to make the corresponding noise. Continue with *Look! A horse. What can you hear?* Again the children should make the animal noise. Repeat the procedure for the five animals (cow, horse, pig, dog and cat).

ACTIVITY 2
- Tell the children they are going to learn a song about the farm animals. First have them listen and identify the animals mentioned in the song.

R·29 🎧

I've got a cow,	I've got a pig,
Moo! Moo! Moo!	Oink! Oink! Oink!
Well, what a noise!	Well, what a noise!
Moo! Moo! Moo!	Oink! Oink! Oink!
I've got a horse,	Yes girls and boys,
Neigh! Neigh! Neigh!	What a noise!
Well, what a noise!	What a noise,
Neigh! Neigh! Neigh!	Girls and boys!

- Play the song again, encouraging the children to join in with the animal noises, and then a third time to sing along.

Ending the lesson

- **EVALUATION:** Ask the children which animals in the picture on page 45 often live with people in their homes (the dog and the cat) and if they themselves have any pets. Let the children talk in L1 about their own pets, or pets that their family or friends have. Now ask them which pets they think Banana and Chocolate have. Hand out the photocopies of page 86. Tell the children to look carefully at the picture and ask them what they think Banana and Chocolate are doing (Banana is holding something in his arms - a cat?, Chocolate has got a lead with something pulling him on the end – a dog?). They should listen to you and then draw Banana and Chocolate's animals in the corresponding spaces. Say: *Banana's got a cat. Chocolate's got a dog.* As the children work go round the class asking: *What's (Chocolate) got?* And: *What's this?* Use this as an opportunity to evaluate the progress of several children.

Reinforcement activity

- Have the children listen to your instructions and circle the animals on page 45 of the *Pupil's Book.* Say: *Draw a circle around the (dog).* The children listen and circle the appropriate animal.

Extension activity

- Make a class graph of the children's pets. Count the different types of pets the children have and then help represent the information on a bar graph. Let the children draw the corresponding animals on their graphs.

Workbook   Page 33

- Say: *Open your workbooks at page 33.* The children match the two halves of each animal by drawing a line between each. Do the first with the whole class.

Farm animals

OBJECTIVES
- To learn more farm animal vocabulary.
- To revise the numbers one to six.

LANGUAGE
Duck, sheep, rabbit, chick.

RECEPTIVE LANGUAGE
Find the (horse). Point to the (sheep).

REVISION
The numbers one to six. *How many (dogs)?*

MATERIALS
Personalised puppets. *Farm Animals poster.* A set of cutout cards from page 51 of the *Pupil's Book.*

Beginning the lesson

- Begin the lesson with the song from the previous lesson (R – 29). Have the children sing along and make the animal noises.

Developing the lesson

- Put up the *poster* and give the children a few moments to look at it. Ask them what they can see (Banana and Chocolate on the farm with lots of different animals). Invite individual children to come to the *poster* and find the animals from lesson 1. Say: *Find the horse!* Continue with *pig, dog* and *cows*.

- Ask the children to listen very carefully. Make the sound of ducks quacking and ask the children to come and find these animals on the *poster*. When they have identified the ducks say: *Yes! Ducks!* Repeat the procedure for *chicks* and *sheep*. Finally show the children the rabbits and say: *Look! Rabbits!*

- Say: *Open your books at pages 46 and 47.* Take the children to the column on the left of page 46 and point to the cow. Ask: *What's this?* Elicit: *Cow* from the children. Repeat for *horse, pig,* and *dog*. Now hand out the personalised puppets and show the children the animals in the column on page 47. Say: *Point to the (sheep).* Continue with *duck, chick* and *rabbit*. Then repeat, saying the names of the animals at random. The children listen again and point with their puppets.

- Stick the horse cutout card on the board and write the number 1 underneath. Point to the horse in the picture on pages 46 and 47 and say: *Look! One horse!* Now stick the dog card on the board and ask: *How many dogs?* Have the children look in their books and tell you *(one)*. Repeat for the pig *(one)*, the cows *(two)*, the sheep *(three)*, the rabbits *(four)*, the chicks *(five)* and the ducks *(six)*. Go through the animals and the numbers on the board, the children repeat after you.

Ending the lesson

- Remove the number six from the board and ask: *How many ducks?* eliciting the answer from the children. Remove the number five and ask: *How many chicks? How many ducks?* eliciting the answers from the children. Continue with the rest of the numbers, and then ask about the animals at random.

Reinforcement activity

- Have the children look at the *poster* and ask: *How many (cows)?* The children answer *two*. Then continue and say the number *(three)*, the children tell you the corresponding animals *(sheep)*.

Extension activity

- Draw the following large animals on the board: a cow, a horse, a sheep and a pig. Give instructions to individual children, saying: *Rub out the (cow's) (eyes),* etc. The children come to the board and remove the corresponding body parts. (Use *eyes, nose, mouth* and *legs*).

Workbook
Page **34**

- Say: *Open your workbooks at page 34.* Show the children the pictures of the dogs, and say: *Look! A big dog, a small dog, a big dog ...* Ask the children what comes next (a small dog). They draw a small dog in the space. The children then complete the series for the other three animals.

Farm animals

OBJECTIVES

- To identify animals from the noises they make.

LANGUAGE

The animal vocabulary learnt so far.

RECEPTIVE LANGUAGE

Be a (cow) (number ones). Run, rabbits! Jump, horses! Stop, rabbits! Run, horses!

REVISION

The numbers one to six. Action verbs.

MATERIALS

Personalised puppets. Scissors.

Beginning the lesson

- Divide the class into six groups and give each group a number from one to six. Give instructions to the class, only the group named should respond with the appropriate animal noise. Say: *Be a cow, (number ones). Be a pig, number threes,* etc.

Developing the lesson

- Have the children open their *Pupil's Books* at pages 46 and 47. Hand out the personalised puppets, and say: *Point to the (cows)!* The children listen and point with their puppets to the main picture.

- Explain to the children that they are going to listen to some of the animals in the picture on pages 46 and 47. They identify the animal from the noise it makes and tell you which it is. Play the recording, stopping after each animal sound, and encourage the children to name the animal. Then play the answer on the recording.

R•30

1. /sound of a pig oinking/
   Narrator: It's a pig.

2. /sound of a duck quacking/
   N: It's a duck.

3. /sound of a horse neighing/
   N: It's a horse.

4. /sound of a sheep baaing/
   N: It's a sheep.

5. /sound of a chick cheeping/
   N: It's a chick.

6. /sound of a dog barking/
   N: It's a dog.

7. /sound of a cow mooing/
   N: It's a cow.

- Hand out the scissors and take the children to the cutout cards on page 51. Instruct them to cut out and prepare their cards, as outlined in previous units. Have the children place their cards in front of them and play the recording (R - 30) again. As the children listen they should hold up the corresponding card. Invite the children

to name the animals. In L1 ask the children which animal they haven't heard (the rabbit). Invite the children to suggest different noises that rabbits might make.

- If you don't plan to do the last two activities in this lesson, collect in the sets of cutout cards now. The children will need them again for lesson 6.

Ending the lesson

- Say: *Stand up. Run!* Have the class running on the spot, then teach the instruction *Stop!* by putting out your hand and arm. Continue with *Jump!* And then *Stop!* Divide the class into two groups, rabbits and horses. Give the instructions: *Run, rabbits! Jump, horses! Stop, rabbits! Run, horses!* etc., changing the instructions for the two animal groups.

Reinforcement activity

- The children need their animal cutout cards for this activity. Have the children work in pairs. They take it in turns to remove one of the cards from their pack and show the rest of their cards to their partner, who tries to guess the missing animal.

Extension activity

- Have the children play in groups of four with their animal cutout cards. Show the children how to start by saying: *The farmer's got a horse,* placing the horse card down on the table. The next child continues with: *The farmer's got a horse and a ...* and chooses one of his or her cards to place next to the horse. The children continue round the group until all the animals have been named.

orkbook   Page **35**

- Say: *Open your workbooks at page 35.* Have the children look carefully at the puzzle to find where the missing pieces go, and then draw a line to the corresponding space.

Farm animals

LESSON 4

OBJECTIVES
- To learn the numbers *seven* and *eight*.
- To revise colours.
- To develop perception skills.

LANGUAGE
Seven, eight.

RECEPTIVE LANGUAGE
If you're wearing something (blue) (stand up). How many chicks can you see? Touch your nose. Turn around. I'm fine. How are you?

REVISION
The numbers one to six. Colours.

MATERIALS
Pencils.

Beginning the lesson

- Revise the colours the children have learnt. Say: *If you're wearing something (blue) stand up*. Go through the colours (black, brown, yellow, white, purple, orange, green, red) until all the children are standing. Then repeat the process saying: *If you're wearing something (purple) sit down,* until all the children are sitting down.

Developing the lesson

- Write the numbers 1 to 6 on the board and ask individual children to come to the board and circle the numbers. Say: *(Juan), circle number three,* etc. Remove the numbers and start to write the numbers on the board beginning at number 1. The children say the numbers as you write. Continue to the number 6. Then add 7 and say: *Look! Seven!* Hold up seven fingers, have the children copy you and say *seven*. Repeat for the number *eight*.

- Say: *Open your books at page 48*. Show the children the numbers at the top of the page and count with the children. Then say: *One is blue*. The children repeat. Continue: *One is blue, two is green,* etc. Teach the children the lines of the following chant and when you get to the actions show the children what to do. Then play the recording for the children to chant along and do the actions. You may wish to break the chant into three stages and teach the children a section at a time.

R•31

One is blue,	Seven is purple,
Two is green.	Eight is blue.
Three is yellow,	I'm fine,
Touch your nose.	/point to yourself/
/touch your nose/	How are you?
	/point to the person next to you/
Four is orange,	
Five is red.	
Six is brown,	
Turn around.	
/turn around on	
the spot/	

Ending the lesson

- **EVALUATION:** Make sure the children all have pencils. Show the children the chicks on page 48 and ask: *How many chicks can you see?* Elicit: *Eight.* Count the chicks with the children. In L1 tell the children to look very carefully at the chicks and to find the ones which are the same. Have the children match the chicks by drawing a line between them. Finally the children trace over the numbers at the bottom of the page. Go round and help where necessary with both activities, using this opportunity to evaluate the work of several children.

Reinforcement activity

- Have the children look at the numbers at the top of page 48. Say: *(Purple)*. The children say: *(Seven)*. Continue with the other colours. (Note both one and eight are blue.) Change around, say the number and the children tell you the colour.

Extension activity

- Practise simple addition sums on the board with the children using the numbers from one to eight. You may wish to do this orally and then have the children write them down.

Workbook   Page **36**

- Say: *Open your workbooks at page 36*. Ask the children if they know who the Easter rabbit is and what he does (he comes at Easter and hides the chocolate eggs). Explain that they are going to colour the Easter rabbit. The children first colour in the patches following your instructions, and then follow the code to colour the rabbit. Say: *One is white, two is yellow, three is brown, four is red*.

Farm animals

OBJECTIVES
* To enjoy listening to a story in English.
* To learn to ask how others are.

LANGUAGE
How are you? I'm fine.

RECEPTIVE LANGUAGE
The (ball's) not here. There's the dog! Here's the ball! The dog's got the ball.

MATERIALS
Banana and Chocolate *flashcards*. A red ball (or the personalised puppets). Scissors. Crayons. Photocopies of the pet pig template (page 87 of the *Resource Bank*). Glue, string.

Beginning the lesson

* Use the Chocolate *flashcard* to ask: *Hello, Banana! How are you?* Banana replies: *I'm fine. How are you?* Use the *flashcards* to ask individual children. Encourage them to reply: *I'm fine. How are you?* Now take the red ball and have the children stand in a circle. Throw the ball to one of the children and ask: *How are you?* The child replies: *I'm fine* and throws the ball to another child and asks: *How are you?* Continue until all the children have had a turn. Alternatively the children can use their personalised puppets and ask and answer with different children in the class.

Developing the lesson

* Ask the children if they know who the red ball belongs to (Chocolate). Let them look at pages 46 and 47 in their *Pupil's Books* to find the ball (in Chocolate's hand). Tell the children that they are going to listen to a story about Chocolate's red ball, and have them come and sit round you in a semi-circle if possible. Show granny at the top of page 49 of the *Pupil's Book*, and ask the children if they are ready for the story.

* Point to the first picture and ask the children what they can see (Banana and Chocolate on the farm with the children and the farmer. Chocolate seems to have a problem.) Ask them what they think is Chocolate's problem (He's lost his ball?) and what is going to happen in the next picture.

* Tell the story, pausing after each picture and inviting the children to predict what will happen next.

R•32

Where's the ball?	picture 3
picture 1	Chocolate: The dog's not here.
Chocolate: Banana, quick! The dog's got the ball!	And the ball's not here. Banana: Look, Chocolate! The dog! Quick!
picture 2	
Banana: The dog's not here. And the ball's not here.	

picture 4
Chocolate: There's the dog!
Running to the pigs!
Banana and Chocolate:
Aaaagh!
Banana: And look! Here's the ball!

* Once you have told the story play the recording and let the children follow in their books. This time stop after each picture and ask the children which animal Banana and Chocolate are with. They can make the corresponding animal noises.

Ending the lesson

* Play the *End of the story* song and encourage the children to sing along.

Reinforcement activity

* Hand out the copies of the pet pig template, the crayons and scissors. (Note: if you are using the *Workbook* you will find this activity on page 37). Ask the children to colour the pig and the circle, and then to cut them out. The children cut along the dotted line inside the circle to make a curly pig's tail. To complete the pet pig, they glue the black dot of the tail to the pig, and then hang it from some string.

Extension activity

* Act out the story (this works best in an open space such as the playground). Divide the class into seven groups, have the groups stand up around the class and allocate names: pigs, sheep, cows, rabbits, chicks and horses. The children make the corresponding noises. Have one child play the part of the dog (give the child the red ball), and two children to play the parts of Banana and Chocolate. Banana and Chocolate cover their eyes whilst the dog hides the ball with one of the groups of animals. Banana and Chocolate then look for the ball in each group. If the group doesn't have the ball the children say: *The ball's not here!* When Banana and Chocolate find the group with the ball they say: *Here's the ball!* Change the children's roles and play again.

Workbook   Page **37**

* Say: *Open your workbooks at page 37.* Hand out scissors and crayons. Ask the children to colour the pig and the circle and then to cut them out. The children then cut along the dotted line inside the circle to make a curly pig's tail. To complete the pet pig they need to glue the black dot of the tail to the pig, and then hang it from some string.

Farm animals

OBJECTIVES
- To revise and consolidate the key language from the unit.
- To provide an opportunity for the children to reflect on the things they have done in the unit.
- To recognise that animals are important for us and that we should respect and care for them.

MATERIALS
Farm Animals poster. The sets of animal cutout cards from lesson 3. Star stickers (one per child). Photocopies of the *Revision Sheet for Unit 6* (see *Evaluation* page 103).

Beginning the lesson

- Put up the *poster*. Give instructions for the children to find the different animals on the *poster*. Say: *Find (a rabbit)*. The children go to the *poster* and point to the corresponding animal(s).

- In L1 ask the children why we look after animals on farms. Establish that we need animals for different products. Invite the children to tell you any of the things that they know come from animals, such as milk, eggs, meat, wool, etc. Remind the children that we should respect and treat animals with care since they are important for us.

Developing the lesson

- Hand out the sets of animal cutouts and play card game 8 on page 77 of the *Resource Bank*.

- Take the children to **My English dictionary** on page 50. Play the recording of the animal vocabulary, the children listen and point in their books. Then go through the pictures again and elicit the language from the children.

R•33

- Cow, horse, pig, dog, rabbit, duck.
- Look! Chicks! One, two, three, four, five, six, seven, eight chicks.
- Sheep.

- **SELF-EVALUATION:** Tell the children they have worked well in this unit and show them their gold stars. Say: *Take a star and stick it here,* pointing to the end of Banana's magic wand on page 50. Then play the *Yaka Boo!* chant and encourage the children to join in.

Ending the lesson

- Hand out the children's envelopes so they can store their cards. Remind the children to clip the set together with a paper clip to help keep them organised.

END OF UNIT EVALUATION

- Hand out the photocopies of the *Revision Sheet for Unit 6*, which can be found on page 103. The indications on how to carry out the evaluation are outlined on page 96.

Food

OBJECTIVES
- To learn some fruit vocabulary.
- To think about the fruits that one likes.
- To recognise that it is important to eat fruit to be strong and healthy.

LANGUAGE
Apple, pear, orange, strawberry.

RECEPTIVE LANGUAGE
Who can you see? Which fruit?

REVISION
Animal vocabulary from unit 6. A set of family member cutouts from unit 3. Family vocabulary from unit 3.

MATERIALS
A set of animal cutout cards from unit 6. A set of family member cutouts from unit 3. Stickers for this lesson. Banana and Chocolate *flashcards*. Sheets of paper and crayons.

Beginning the lesson

- Have a child come to the front and show him or her an animal card without letting the other children see it. The child mimes the animal without making a sound. The other children have to guess the animal. Repeat with the different animals learnt in unit 6, and different children miming.

Developing the lesson

- Use the Banana and Chocolate *flashcards* to ask the children: *How are you?* Encourage the children to reply: *I'm fine, how are you?* Then use Banana to tell the children that some members of his family are on page 53 in their books, and have the children guess who (his brother and sister). Elicit the different family members from unit 3 (*father, mother, brother, sister* and *baby*) and draw them on the board, or stick the cutout cards on the board. Ask the children to look again at page 53 to guess what Banana's brother and sister are doing (flying kites). Ask whether they have kites or have ever been to fly a kite.

- Point to the sister's kite, indicate the apple and say: *Look! An apple!* Repeat for *pear* and *orange*. Have the children repeat the names of the fruits with you. Then invite the children to find the other fruits in the picture, and teach the word *strawberry*. (Some of the children may suggest *banana*.)

- Explain to the children that Banana's sister likes apples, pears and oranges. Play the first part of the recording (the sister speaking) for the children to listen and follow on page 53. Stop after each fruit is named for the children to point in their books.

R•34

Sister:
I like apples. Yum! Yum!
And, I like pears!
And, I like oranges! Yummy!
Yummy! Yummy!

Brother:
I like apples too! Yum! Yum!
Yum!

And, I like pears!
And, I like strawberries,
I like yummy, yummy
strawberries!

Sister and brother:
What fruits do you like?

- Hand out the sheets of paper and ask the children to guess which three fruits Banana's brother likes and to draw them on the sheet of paper (they should choose from apple, pear, orange and strawberry). Go over the drawings with the children, then play the second part of the recording for them to check. Stop after each fruit and ask the children: *Which fruit?* See if any of the children guessed correctly and say: *Well done!* Play the final question on the recording for the children. Encourage them to tell you the fruits they like from the ones shown on page 53. Finally emphasise to the children the importance of eating fruit to be strong and healthy.

Ending the lesson

- **EVALUATION:** Show the children the stickers for this lesson. The children complete Banana's brother's kite by sticking on the corresponding fruits. As they work go round the class asking individual children to name the fruits and check on several children's progress.

Reinforcement activity

- Mime preparing and eating the different fruits from page 53. The children guess which fruit it is.

Extension activity

- Say the colours of the fruits learnt in this lesson, the children guess which fruit it is.

Workbook   Page 39

- Say: *Open your workbooks at page 39.* Ask the children to name the fruits they can see on the page and then to colour them in the following colours: apples - red; oranges - orange; pears - green; strawberries - red. The children then count the fruits and write the number in the corresponding square. (Key: 4 pears, 5 apples, 8 oranges, 7 strawberries.).

Food

LESSON 2

OBJECTIVES
- To learn more fruit vocabulary.
- To revise the numbers one to eight.

LANGUAGE
Lemon, banana. Yes! No! It's a (pear)!

RECEPTIVE LANGUAGE
Who is in the bed? Look at the bed! How many apples?

REVISION
The numbers one to eight.

MATERIALS
A bag of fruit with an apple, a pear, a strawberry, an orange, a lemon and a banana. A set of fruit cutout cards from page 59 of the *Pupil's Book*. Personalised puppets. Sheets of paper and crayons.

Beginning the lesson

- Have the bag of fruit ready with the apple, pear, orange and strawberry. Invite the children to come and feel the fruit (tell them to be careful so as not to squash the strawberry!). Ask them to choose one and say what it is. (Alternatively have the four corresponding cutout cards turned face down, the children take a card and name the fruit.) Ask: *Do you like (apples)?*, and encourage the children to reply *Yes* or *No*.

Developing the lesson

- Now teach the two new fruits, *lemon* and *banana,* either with the real fruits or with the cards. Show the fruits and name them, the children repeat after you. Say: *Open your books at pages 54 and 55.* Give the children a few minutes to look at the picture and then ask them about it. Ask: *Who is in the bed?* eliciting the names of the six fruits *(lemon, orange, strawberry, pear, banana* and *apple).* Now hand out the personalised puppets and show the children the two columns on the right and left. Say: *Point to the (strawberry). Point to the (orange).* Go through the six fruits at random.

- Stick the banana cutout card on the board. Pointing to the *Pupil's Book* say: *Look at the bed! How many bananas?* The children count the bananas on the bedspread in the main picture (not in the bed). Write 3 on the board under the banana. Stick another fruit card on the board and continue in the same way for all six fruits (4 oranges, 5 apples, 6 pears, 7 lemons, 8 strawberries).

Ending the lesson

- Use your set of fruit cutout cards. Hold up the (apple) and say: *Look! An apple!* Encourage the children to say *Yes!* Then hold up the pear and say: *Look! (A strawberry!)* Encourage the children to say *No!* and correct you with: *It's a pear.*

Reinforcement activity

- Hand out sheets of paper and crayons. The children draw themselves eating their favourite fruit from the six fruits they have learnt.

Extension activity

- Prepare a class graph of favourite fruits. Go through the six fruits and count the children's favourites. Then prepare the results on a bar chart. Have the children decorate the graphs with drawings of the fruits and display on the walls.

Workbook   Page **40**

- Say: *Open your workbooks at page 40.* The children observe the two pictures carefully and find and circle the differences. (Key: **Picture 1**: 8 strawberries, 7 apples and 4 lemons on the stall. Banana has an apple, his sister has an orange and the baby has a strawberry; **Picture 2**: 6 strawberries, 8 apples and 5 lemons on the stall. Banana has an orange, his sister has a strawberry and the baby has an apple.)

Food

Objectives
- To learn the unit song.
- To consolidate the fruit vocabulary.

Receptive language
Look! It's a (lemon). (Six) fruits in the bed. Roll over! So they all roll over and the (apple) falls out.

Revision
The numbers one to six.

Materials
A set of fruit cutout cards. The bag of fruit from the previous lesson. Sheets of paper.

Beginning the lesson

- Use either the bag of fruit or the cards. Show either a fruit or a card and say: *Look! It's a (lemon).* Make true and false statements about the fruits / cards. The children stand up if the statements are true, but remain seated if they are false.

Developing the lesson

- Have the children open their *Pupil's Books* at pages 54 and 55 and take them to the fruits in the bed. Elicit the fruits from the children, from left to right. Ask them why the banana and the apple are frightened (because there is a very sleepy mouse wanting to get in the bed!) Then ask the children what they think would happen if the fruits rolled over in the bed (they would probably fall out). Tell the children they are going to learn a song about the fruits in the bed. Tell them that this is exactly what happens, the lemon tells them to roll over and the fruits at the other end fall onto the floor. First play the song and let the children listen and follow in their books. Point to the fruits in your book during the song.

R•35

Six fruits in the bed and the lemon says, Roll over, roll over! So they all roll over and the apple falls out. Ouch!	Three fruits in the bed and the lemon says, Roll over! Roll over! So they all roll over and the strawberry falls out. Ouch!
Five fruits in the bed and the lemon says, Roll over, roll over! So they all roll over and the banana falls out. Ouch!	Two fruits in the bed and the lemon says, Roll over, roll over! So they both roll over and the orange falls out. Ouch!
Four fruits in the bed and the lemon says, Roll over, roll over! So they all roll over and the pear falls out. Ouch!	One fruit in the bed and the lemon says, Roll over, roll over! So the lemon rolls over and the lemon falls out! Ouch! Ouch! Ouch!

- Play the song a second time for the children to join in.
- Now act out the song. Divide the class into groups of six and allocate the roles of the six fruits to the members of each group (if your class doesn't divide into groups of six, children can double up roles in the groups). Have the children form a line in their group, making the same order as the fruits in the bed. Go through each fruit checking that the children know who they are. As the children listen and sing the song the first child (the lemon) shouts: *Roll over, roll over* and the other children turn around. The end fruit 'falls out' and shouts: *Ouch!* Play the song and have the children act it out.

Ending the lesson

- Have the children leave the class by saying: *Pears can go! Lemons can go!*, etc.

Reinforcement activity

- Display a selection of the fruits (or cutout cards) to the children. Give them a minute to look and then cover up the fruits / cards. The children try to remember what they have seen.

Extension activity

- Hand out sheets of paper and do the following dictation. Say: *Draw a table. Draw a lemon on the table. Draw two bananas on the table. Draw four apples on the table. Draw six strawberries on the table. Now draw a mouse eating one of the strawberries!*

Workbook   Page 41

- Say: *Open your workbooks at page 41.* Have the children name the six fruits on the page and then the six parts of the body they are touching. Have the children stand up. Go through the instructions saying: *Touch your (eyes)*, etc. Then say: *(Pear!)* The children look at their books and do the same action as the pear. Repeat for the different fruits.

Food

OBJECTIVES
- To learn the numbers *nine* and *ten*.
- To extract specific information from a listening text.

LANGUAGE
Nine, ten.

RECEPTIVE LANGUAGE
Mmm, (oranges). I like (oranges). (Eight oranges) for me. What fruit do you like? What fruit don't you like? Stand up! Be (happy!)

REVISION
The numbers one to eight. Members of the family.

MATERIALS
Pencils, crayons and sheets of paper.

Beginning the lesson

- Have the children chant the numbers from one to eight and then count down from eight to one (you may need to write them on the board). Show the children nine fingers and say: *Look! Nine!* Have the children copy you holding up nine fingers. Then suddenly make the tenth one appear and say: *Oh, ten!* In a voice of surprise. Do this with the children. They should reveal their fingers one by one, counting at the same time. When they get to nine they should pause, and then suddenly make the tenth appear and say: *Ten!*

Developing the lesson

- Have the children open their *Pupil's Books* at page 56. Give them a few seconds to look at the pictures and then point to the baskets of fruit and the numbers across the top of the page. Have the children relate the fruits in the basket with the numbers at the top. Say: *Six?* The children point to and say: *Apples.* Repeat for the other numbers and fruits. (6 apples, 7 lemons, 8 oranges, 9 pears and 10 strawberries).

- Now elicit the family members on the left of the page *(father, mother, baby, brother, sister)*. Tell the children they are going to listen to Banana's family talking about the fruits on the right. As the children listen they should draw a line to connect the 'person' with his / her basket of fruit. Play the recording, stopping after each one for the children to draw the line. Go over the answer before continuing.

R•36

Banana's father:
Mmm, oranges. I like oranges. Eight oranges for me.

Banana's mother:
Mmm, lemons. I like lemons. Seven lemons for me.

The baby:
Mmm, strawberries. I like strawberries. Ten strawberries

for me!

Banana's brother:
Mmm, apples. I like apples. Six apples for me.

Banana's sister:
Mmm, pears. I like pears. Nine pears for me.

- Finally the children complete the numbers from six to ten at the bottom of the page by tracing over the dots.

Ending the lesson

- **EVALUATION:** Make sure the children all have crayons and sheets of paper. Ask the children to draw two plates, on one plate they draw a fruit they like, and on the other, a fruit that they don't like. As the children are working go round and ask: *What fruit do you like? What fruit don't you like?* Use this as an opportunity to evaluate the progress of several children.

Reinforcement activity

- Give the following instructions to the children, say: *Stand up! Be happy!* Then say: *Be sad!* The children mime the different emotions. Now name the six fruits that the children have learnt, if they like them they show a happy face, if they don't like them they show a sad face.

Extension activity

- Do some sums on the board working with the numbers from one to ten. Use both addition and subtraction. Have the children give you the answers orally.

Workbook
Page **42**

- Say: *Open your workbooks at page 42.* Do a drawing dictation of the fruits that Banana and Chocolate like / dislike. Say: *Banana likes apples, strawberries and oranges. He doesn't like pears. Chocolate likes strawberries, oranges and pears. He doesn't like lemons.* The children listen and draw the fruits on the corresponding plates.

OBJECTIVES
- To enjoy listening to a story in English.
- To revise the parts of the face.

LANGUAGE
Pizza.

RECEPTIVE LANGUAGE
I like pizza. I'm hungry (too). Show me your (eyes). Do you like pizza?

REVISION
Parts of the face vocabulary.

MATERIALS
Flashcards: Chocolate, pizza. Photocopies of page 88 of the *Resource Bank* or the children's personalised puppets. Scissors, crayons and string. Sheets of paper.

Beginning the lesson

- Say: *Stand up!*, and play *Chocolate Says* with the children, using: *Show me your eyes / nose / mouth!*

Developing the lesson

- Show the children the *flashcard* of the pizza and ask: *What's this?* eliciting: *Pizza* from the children. Ask: *Do you like pizza?* Encourage the children to respond *Yes* or *No.* Tell the children that Banana and Chocolate like pizza a lot, and that today they are going to hear a story about Banana and Chocolate, and a very special pizza. Explain that Banana and Chocolate are very hungry, teaching the expression *I'm hungry.* Have the children come and sit round you in a semi-circle if possible. Show granny at the top of page 57 of the *Pupil's Book*, and ask the children if they are ready for the story.

- Point to the first picture and ask the children what they can see (Chocolate is leaving the kitchen carefully carrying a pizza). Ask the children where they think he is going (to the dining room) and what he is going to do (eat the pizza). Ask the children if they think he's going to eat it all himself or share it with Banana.

- Tell the story, pausing after each picture and inviting the children to predict what will happen next.

R•37

Banana and Chocolate's pizza!

picture 1
Chocolate: Mmm, pizza. I like pizza. Oh, I'm hungry.

picture 2
Banana: Mmm, pizza. Yummy, yummy pizza. I'm hungry too! Wait for me, Chocolate!

picture 3
Banana: Look, Chocolate! Two eyes, a nose and a mouth! He he he!
Chocolate: He he he he he he!

picture 4
Pizza: Oh no, oh no, oh no!
You're not eating me!
Goodbye, Banana!
Goodbye, Chocolate!

- Once you have told the story play the recording and let the children follow in their books.

- Now act out the story. First let the children decide the part they would like to play (Chocolate, Banana, or the pizza), or allocate the roles. Hand out the photocopies of page 88 (the story characters). Help the children colour them and cut them out, and then put the string through and tie to hang round their necks. Teach the actions with the following lines:

  I'm hungry. /they rub their tummies/

  Two eyes, a nose and a mouth! /they indicate these parts of their face/

  Goodbye Banana! Goodbye Chocolate! /they pretend to run away, waving at the same time/

- Play the story again, pausing after each line for the corresponding children to repeat and do the actions. (Alternatively the children can use their personalised puppets.)

Ending the lesson

- Play the *End of the story* song and encourage the children to sing along.

Reinforcement activity

- Have the children play the following game in groups. They take turns to mime eating one of the fruits they have learnt in the unit, or the pizza. The other children guess what they are eating.

Extension activity

- Hand out sheets of paper and do a fruit dictation, including different face and body parts. Say: *Draw a banana. Draw two eyes, a nose and a mouth. Draw two legs, and two arms.* Continue for different fruits or a pizza.

Workbook   Page 43

- Say: *Open your workbooks at page 43.* The children first number the pictures at the top of the page in the order of the story. In the second activity the children find the two pizzas which are the same. (Key: pizzas 2 and 5).

Food

OBJECTIVES

- To revise and consolidate the key language from the unit.
- To recognise the importance of eating fruit.
- To provide an opportunity for the children to reflect on the things they have done in the unit.

MATERIALS

Star stickers (one per child). Scissors. Paper plates or sheets of paper. Photocopies of the *Revision Sheet for Unit 7* (see *Evaluation* page 104). Chocolate *flashcard*.

Beginning the lesson

- Hand out the scissors and take the children to page 59 of the *Pupil's Book*. Have the children cut out and prepare the fruit cutout cards as in previous lessons. Name each fruit and have the children hold up the corresponding card.

Developing the lesson

- **EVALUATION:** Now hand out two paper plates to each child, have them draw a happy face on one, and a sad face on the other. (Alternatively hand out sheets of paper.) Have the children place their fruit cards on one of the plates according to whether they like or dislike the fruit. As the children work, go round and have the children name the fruits they like / don't like. Say: *What fruits do you like? What fruits don't you like?* Use this as an opportunity to evaluate the progress of several children. Finally emphasise the importance of eating fruit to be healthy and strong to the children. Keep the plates for the next unit.

- Now play card game 9 on page 77 of the *Resource Bank*.

- Take the children to **My English dictionary** on page 58. Play the recording of the food and numbers vocabulary, the children listen and point in their books. Then go through the pictures again and elicit the language from the children.

R•38

- Pear, orange, banana, lemon, apple, pizza.
- Look! Strawberries. One, two, three, four, five, six, seven, eight, nine, ten strawberries.
- Look! The mouse is in the bed!

- Finally ask the children: *Where's the mouse?* Elicit: **In the bed**. Ask the children to go back to page 42 in their *Pupil's Books* and to find the mouse. Ask again: *Where's the mouse?* Encourage the children to say: **On the table**. Make sure all the children have their pencil at hand and play *Chocolate Says* using: *Put your pencil in your bag / on the table / in your book / on the floor.*

- **SELF-EVALUATION:** Tell the children they have worked very well in this unit and show them their gold stars. Say: *Take a star and stick it here*, pointing to the words *Yaka Boo!* on page 58. Then play the *Yaka Boo!* chant and encourage the children to join in.

Ending the lesson

- Hand out the children's envelopes so they can store their cards. Remind the children to clip the set together with a paper clip to help keep them organised.

END OF UNIT EVALUATION

- Hand out the photocopies of the *Revision Sheet for Unit 7*, which can be found on page 104. The indications on how to carry out the evaluation are outlined on page 97.

Workbook   Page **44**

- Say: *Open your workbooks at page 44.* Play *Fruit Bingo*. The children draw between one and three more fruits on the respective trays. Now call out the fruits using numbers between one and four. Say: *Three apples, two bananas*, etc. If the children have the same number on their tray they shout *Bingo!* Check their drawings. Continue until one of the children has *Bingo* for all the trays.

Let's play!

LESSON 1

OBJECTIVES
- To introduce transport vocabulary.
- To learn the unit chant.

LANGUAGE
Car, lorry, bike. In the (car). On the bike.

RECEPTIVE LANGUAGE
Go! Stop! Where's (Banana)? Look! She's in the lorry!

REVISION
Up and down. Yes! No!

MATERIALS
Flashcards: Banana, Chocolate, bike, car. Sheets of paper and crayons.

Beginning the lesson

- Explain to the children in L1 that they are coming to the end of the course, and that they are now going to play in English. Put the bike and the car *flashcards* on the board and, using the Banana and Chocolate *flashcards*, say: *Look! A bike! Look! A car!* Divide the class into Banana's team and Chocolate's team and let them decide what they would like to be, a car or a bike. Banana and Chocolate then give the instruction: *Go!* The children move round the classroom as either cars or bikes. Give the instruction: *Stop!*, raising your arm and hand at the same time. The children should 'freeze'. Should anybody move they are out of the game. Continue with: *Go!* The team left with most members is the winner. (If you don't have much space in the classroom the children can move 'on the spot'.)

- **NOTE:** A variation of the game, and slightly more complex, is to have Banana give instructions to his team while Chocolate gives instructions to his. The children should be careful to follow only their own team's instructions.

Developing the lesson

- Say: *Open your books at page 61.* Have the children look at the page and ask: *Where's Banana? Where's Chocolate?* Encourage the children to reply: *In the car.* Point to the boy behind and ask: *Where's the boy?* Elicit: *On the bike.* Finally ask: *Where's the girl?* Point to the girl and say: *Look! She's in the lorry!* Now say the names of the three vehicles. The children listen and point, and then listen and repeat.

- Tell the children that they are going to learn a chant about the children playing with Banana and Chocolate. Play the chant and have them mime the actions (riding a bike, driving a car, driving a lorry). Then play the recording again for the children to chant along.

R•39 🎧

Boy:	Girl:
On the bike,	In the lorry,
Tring, tring, tring.	Toot, toot, toot.
Up and down,	Up and down,
On the bike!	In the lorry!
Banana and Chocolate:	
In the car,	
Vroom, vroom, vroom.	
Up and down,	
In the car!	

Ending the lesson

- Make true and false statements about the picture. Say: *Banana and Chocolate are in the car.* The children say: *Yes!* and stand up. Say: *The girl is on the bike.* The children say *No!* and remain seated. Continue with different statements.

Reinforcement activity

- Play a miming game: Say: *Lorries!* The children mime being lorries. Do the same for *car* and *bike.*

Extension activity

- Do a picture dictation. Hand out sheets of paper and instruct the children to draw the three vehicles but adding adjectives of colour and size, for example: *Draw a big yellow lorry. Draw a small purple bike. Draw a big green car.*

TEACHING NOTES

Let's play!

OBJECTIVES

- To learn some toy vocabulary.
- To recognise the importance of tidying up the class after working and playing.

LANGUAGE

Teddy bear, ball, doll.

RECEPTIVE LANGUAGE

Can you find the cars?

REVISION

The numbers from one to six.

MATERIALS

Personalised puppets. A set of the toy cutout cards from page 67 of the *Pupil's Book*.

Beginning the lesson

- Tell the children that today they are going to learn about Banana and Chocolate's toys. Show the three vehicle cutout cards and elicit the names from the children. Then mix them up and stick them face down on the board. Write a number under each from one to three. The children give you a number and try to guess the corresponding card. If they are correct show them the card.
- Now present *doll, teddy bear* and *ball* with the cutout cards. Say the words and have the children repeat with you.

Developing the lesson

- Hand out the personalised puppets and say: *Open your books at pages 62 and 63.* Give the children a few minutes to look at the picture and say: *Take your puppets, point to Banana and Chocolate.* Show the children the transport vehicles in the column on the left of page 62 and say: *Point to the lorry. Point to the bike. Point to the car.* Repeat, saying the words at random. Continue in the same way with *teddy bear, ball* and *doll* from the column on page 63.
- Now tell the children that they are going to listen to some questions about the main picture. They should listen carefully and try to find the different toys. First do an example with the children. Say: *Can you find the cars?* The children look for the cars in the main picture and point with their puppets. Have the children listen to the recording, stopping after each question to give the children time to find the toy(s). For the final question make squeaking noises to give the children a clue!

R•40

Can you find the cars?	Can you find the ball?
Can you find the lorries?	Can you find the doll?
Can you find the bike?	Can you find the teddy bear?
	Can you find the mouse?

- Ask the children what is happening in the main picture (the teacher is asking Banana and Chocolate to tidy up the toys). See if the children can tell you why it is important to tidy up after playing or working in the classroom.

Ending the lesson

- Play the game from *Beginning the lesson* but this time with all six cutout cards. Write the numbers from one to six underneath the cards as you stick them at random, face down, on the board.

Reinforcement activity

- 🎧 Play the chant from lesson 1 (R - 39) and have the children do the actions. If you have enough space you can let the children move up and down the classroom as they chant.

Extension activity

- Point to the mouse on pages 62 and 63 and say: *Look! The mouse is under the book.* Draw three pictures on the board, a mouse on a table, a mouse under a book, and a mouse in a bed. Go through each saying: *Look! A mouse on the table!*, etc. Invite individual children to come and rub out the pictures. Say: *Rub out the mouse (under) the (book)!* Then invite the children to come and draw the mice in the same positions.

Workbook   Page 45

- Say: *Open your workbooks at page 45.* Give the children a few moments to look carefully at the page and then go through the different toys on the page. Tell the children that Banana and Chocolate have been playing and that it is time to tidy up. The children help Banana and Chocolate to put the things in the correct boxes. Have the children draw a line to connect the toys with the corresponding toy box. Go round helping where necessary. The children can then colour the toys.

KEY: car, bike and lorry in the 'car' box; fruit in the 'shop' box; dolls and teddy bears in the 'teddy bear' box; the hat and wand in the 'clothes' box.

Let's play!

OBJECTIVES

- To consolidate the toy vocabulary learnt so far.
- To revise key language from previous units.

RECEPTIVE LANGUAGE

Jump to the board for ... the teddy bear. Find the pigs.

REVISION

Vocabulary items from units one to seven.

MATERIALS

A set of toy cutout cards. The personalised puppets. A list of vocabulary you wish to revise from the items on pages 62 and 63. Banana and Chocolate *flashcards*. Scissors.

Beginning the lesson

- Play the following game with the toy cutout cards. Alternatively, if you feel the children are confident with the new language, use cutout cards from a previous unit for revision. Stick the set of cards on the board and divide the class into two teams. Have the two teams standing behind an imaginary line, and make space so they can get to the board easily. Now call out one of the words on the board, saying: *Jump to the board for ... the teddy bear.* One child from each team jumps to the board and tries to take the corresponding card first. Repeat until all the cards have been 'won'.

Developing the lesson

- Hand out the personalised puppets and have the children open their *Pupil's Books* at pages 62 and 63. Give instructions for the children to find different things in the main picture with their puppet. Say: *Find the pigs. Find the pizzas,* etc. choosing from your vocabulary list.

- **EVALUATION:** Give the children the scissors and take them to page 67. The children cut out and prepare the cards as described in previous units. Go through the toys and have the children listen and hold up the corresponding card. Now have the children play the *Memory Game* in pairs. They mix up their two sets of cards and place them face down on the desk or table. They then try to find two matching cards, taking turns to turn over two cards. If they are the same the children name the toy to be able to keep the cards. The game continues. As they play, go round and evaluate the progress of several children.

NOTE:

If you don't plan to do the reinforcement activity, collect in the sets of cards now. The children will need them again for lesson 6.

Ending the lesson

- Write the following numbers across the board, large and clear: 1, 2, 3, 4, 5, 6, 7. Explain to the children that they should try to find objects in the picture which correspond to these numbers, for example: 2 - there are two cars in the picture. When the children find toys which correspond, invite them to name the toy(s) and to draw them on the board below the number. (1 - doll, teddy bear, ball, apple, bike; 2 - cars; 3 - lorries; 4 - pizzas; 5 - pigs; 6 - pears; 7 - strawberries.)

Reinforcement activity

- Have the children take out their toy cutout cards. They listen and place them in the order that you give them. Say: *One, the doll. Two, the bike,* etc.

Extension activity

- Stick the Banana *flashcard* on one side of the room, and the Chocolate *flashcard* on the other. Divide the class into six groups and give each group a toy name from the six items learnt. Now say: *Banana's got a ball. Chocolate's got a bike,* etc. The 'ball' children should go and stand in the corresponding part of the room. Repeat for the other toys. Have the children change names and play again.

Workbook   Page 46

- Say: *Open your workbooks at page 46.* Ask the children what they can see on the page (a present). The children count the balls, the dolls and the teddy bears on the wrapping paper and then write the numbers in the corresponding boxes. Finally ask the children who they want to give the present to, and help them write the name on the tag.

KEY: 8 balls; 10 dolls; 9 teddy bears.

Let's play!

LESSON 4

OBJECTIVES
- To revise key language items from units one to eight.

RECEPTIVE LANGUAGE
Move your (feet) like a robot. What's this number? Stick the number three here. Goodbye number (twos).

REVISION
Parts of the body. Language from units one to eight.

MATERIALS
Stickers for this lesson. Counters and coins or dice to play the board game.

Beginning the lesson

- Revise the parts of the body with the *Robot Game.* Give the children instructions to move different parts of their body. They should try to imitate robots. Say: *Move your (feet) like a robot.* Repeat with the different parts of the body learnt in unit 2.

Developing the lesson

- Say: *Open your books at page 64.* Give the children a few moments to look carefully at the page and then tell the children that they are going to play a board game, but first they have to find the different things on the page. Name some of the objects while the children listen and point.
- **EVALUATION:** Take the children to the stickers which correspond with this page and ask them to say the numbers. Ask: *What's this number?* Elicit: *Three, six, eight* and *ten.* Show the children the empty square next to the chair in the bottom row of the board and say: *Stick the number three here.* Do the same with the other stickers, moving up the board. Now hand out the coins or dice, and the counters. Explain to the children how to play. They place their counters at the beginning of the board on *start* and then throw the dice or coin (heads move forward one square, tails move forward two squares) to move forward. As they land on a square they should name the object. If the children land on Banana's magic wand they can move up to the square indicated, but if they fall on the banana skin, they have to move down to the square indicated. Have the children play in twos or threes. As they play, go round and help where necessary, using this opportunity to evaluate their progress.

Ending the lesson

- Revise the numbers from one to ten with the children, writing them on the board. Have the children choose one of the numbers, and say: *(Twos!) Hands up!* Give instructions for the children to leave saying: *Goodbye number twos. Goodbye number nines,* etc.

Reinforcement activity

- Play one of the songs that the children have learnt through the course and have them sing along.

Extension activity

- Give the children the following instructions: *Put your book under the table. Put your book on the table. Put your book in your bag.* If the children are confident repeat with *pencil, rubber, crayon,* etc.

Let's play!

OBJECTIVES
- To revise the members of the family and language learnt throughout the course.
- To enjoy listening to a story in English.

RECEPTIVE LANGUAGE
Who is it? It's party time. Dance! Come in! Time for chocolate cake! Put the pizza on the table!

REVISION
Members of the family. *Pizza, cake, balloons.*

MATERIALS
Flashcards: pizza, cake, balloon, Banana, Chocolate, Cherry and Ice cream. A set of the fruit cutout cards from unit 7. Some lively music.

Beginning the lesson

- Play *Musical Cards* with the pizza, cake, balloon and the fruit cards. Hand out the cards and play the music, as the children listen they pass the cards round. When the music stops the children holding the cards should stand up and say what they are holding.

Developing the lesson

- Tell the children that Banana and Chocolate are having a very special party today because it's the end of the course, and that they have invited some special friends. Have the children open their *Pupil's Books* at page 65. Give them a few moments to look at the pictures and then ask them what they can see in the first one. (Banana and Chocolate's party. Banana and Chocolate are carefully placing a pizza on the table. Banana's brother and sister and the baby are dancing, the father is watching). Ask who is missing (the mother) and where they think she is (in the kitchen?).
- Now tell the story. Ask the children to listen carefully to see if they can identify Banana and Chocolate's special friends.

R•41

The cake

picture 1
Narrator: It's party time. Dance! Dance! Dance everybody! Banana and Chocolate have got a pizza. On the table! Put the pizza on the table!

picture 2
Banana's mother: Hello Cherry! Hello Ice Cream! Come in, come in!
Cherry and Ice Cream: Hello! Hello!

picture 3
Mother: Time for cake! Time for chocolate cake!

picture 4
Everybody (except the father): Look! Look!

- Ask the children if they can tell you who the friends are (Cherry and Ice Cream), and why everybody laughs in surprise at the end (the father, who has been unable to walk throughout the book because of his broken leg, can suddenly walk!).
- Now play the recording of the story and let the children follow again in their books.

Ending the lesson

- Put the four character *flashcards* on the board and elicit the names from the children. Have them repeat *Cherry* and *Ice Cream*. Tell the children that next year they will see more of Cherry and Ice Cream, who will play and have fun with them in the English class.
- Finish the lesson with the *End of the Story* song.

Reinforcement activity

- Play *Who is it?* with the character *flashcards*. Divide the class into two teams. Stick the cards on the board face down, and then ask individual children: *Who is it?*, pointing to one of the cards. If the child guesses correctly they win a point for their team. Put the card back and mix them up to continue playing.

Extension activity

- Go back to the board game on page 64. Name a category and see if the children can tell you something which belongs to it, say: *Fruits!* The children reply: *Apple / strawberry.* Repeat for the different objects.

Workbook   Page 47

- Ask the children if they know how to play dominoes. Tell them they are going to play toy dominoes in this lesson. Say: *Open your workbooks at page 47.* Hand out the scissors and help the children cut along the dotted lines to make 12 dominoes (there are two images on each domino). When the children are ready have them play in pairs. They share out the dominoes between them and then start to play. As they place a connecting picture on the table, they should name the object. The first child to put down all his or her dominoes wins.

Let's play!

LESSON 6

OBJECTIVES
- To revise and consolidate the key language from the unit.
- To provide an opportunity for the children to reflect on the things they have done in the unit.

RECEPTIVE LANGUAGE
Look! Banana's got a (ball).

MATERIALS
Star stickers (one per child). Banana and Chocolate *flashcards*. The sets of toy cutout cards, plus a set for yourself. Photocopies of the *Revision Sheet for Unit 8* (see *Evaluation* page 105).

Beginning the lesson

- Stick the Banana and Chocolate *flashcards* on the board and take one of the toy cutout cards, saying: *Look! Banana's got a (ball)*. Stick the ball under Banana. Continue with the other *flashcards* but let the children decide who the toys belong to.

Developing the lesson

- **EVALUATION:** Hand out the sets of toy cutout cards. Ask the children to classify the toy cards according to the things that they have or haven't got. Let the children then work in groups to tell the other children about the toys that they have. As the children work go round helping. Use this opportunity to evaluate the progress of the children.
- Now play card game number 10 on page 77 of the *Resource Bank*.
- Take the children to **My English dictionary** on page 66. Play the recording of the toy vocabulary, and have the children listen and point in their books. Then go through the pictures again and elicit the language from the children. Finally, play the last two sentences, pointing to the mouse and the four friends on the page.

R•42

- Lorry, car, bike, ball, doll, teddy bear.
- Look! The mouse is under the book!
- Look! Banana and Chocolate AND Cherry and Ice Cream!

- Tell the children they have worked very well in this unit and show them their gold stars. Say: *Take a star and stick it here,* pointing to the word *Yaka Boo!* on page 66. Then play the *Yaka Boo!* chant and encourage the children to join in.

Ending the lesson

- Hand out the children's envelopes so they can store their cutout cards. Remind the children to clip the set together with a paper clip to help keep them organised.

END OF UNIT EVALUATION

- Hand out the photocopies of the *Revision Sheet for Unit 8*, which can be found on page 105. The indications on how to carry out the evaluation are outlined on page 97.

Happy Birthday

OBJECTIVES
- To learn vocabulary related to birthdays.
- To say how old you are.
- To learn the birthday song.

LANGUAGE
Cake, candle, present, balloon. I'm (six).

RECEPTIVE LANGUAGE
How old are you? How many (cakes) can you see? What is it? If you're (six) you can go.

REVISION
Family members. Numbers. *Ball, book, T-shirt, bike.*

MATERIALS
Flashcards: Banana, Chocolate, present, cake, candle and balloon. A prepared birthday present for Banana, or for one of the children if it is their birthday. Stickers for this lesson. Different coloured balloons (colours which the children have already learnt). Some lively music. Sheets of paper.

- **NOTE:** You may not have covered some of the language which comes up in this lesson, depending on the time of year that you use it. In this case use the L1.

Beginning the lesson

- Use the Banana and Chocolate *flashcards* to greet the children and then have Chocolate turn to Banana and say: *Happy birthday, Banana!* Tell the children that today is Banana's birthday and take out the present. Give it to Banana and invite the children to guess what is inside. Then have the children help Banana open it. Alternatively, if today is one of the children's birthday, give the prepared present to the child and say: *Happy birthday (María).* Invite the rest of the children to join in and say: *Happy birthday!*

Developing the lesson

- Put the cake *flashcard* on the board and say: *Look! A cake!* Continue with *candle, balloon* and *present.* Have the children repeat the words after you. Now ask the children to open their *Pupil's Books* at page 69 and ask them what they can see (Banana's birthday party). Ask the children who is at the party, eliciting: *Chocolate, the mother, father, brother, sister* and *baby.*
- Point to the cake *flashcard* and ask: *How many cakes can you see?* Elicit the answer: *One.* Continue and ask about the balloons *(four),* the presents *(four)* and the candles *(seven).* Finally ask: *How old is Banana?* and point to the candles on the cake. The children count the candles, elicit: *Seven.*

- Say: *Let's sing 'Happy Birthday' to Banana!* Play the recording and have the children sing along. Point to the cake, candle, present and balloon *flashcards* as they come up in the song and encourage the children to do the same.

R•43 🎧

Happy birthday to you,	With cakes and candles,
Happy birthday to you.	Presents and balloons.
Happy birthday, dear Banana,	Happy birthday, dear Banana,
Happy birthday to you.	Happy birthday to you!

- Take the children to the presents in the picture, point to the bike and ask: *What is it?* Have the children try to guess what is in the presents. As they suggest the items, say: *A ball? A bike? A T-shirt? A book?* and draw these things on the board. (Alternatively ask the children to draw their ideas on paper.) Now show the children the stickers for this lesson. Say: *Look! A bike! A ball! A book! And a T-shirt!* The children stick the stickers over the corresponding presents. As the children work go round asking: *What is it?*

Ending the lesson

- Ask individual children: *How old are you?* Group the children according to their ages and let the children leave by saying: *If you're (six) you can go.*

Reinforcement activity

- Hand out sheets of paper. The children draw the present that they would like for their next birthday. Go round and ask the children about the drawings.

Extension activity

- Play *Musical Balloons.* Have the balloons blown up and ready. Play some lively music, the children pass the balloons around in time to the music. Stop the music and ask or say to the children holding the balloons: *What colour is the balloon? How old are you?* or *Name one of Banana's presents.*

Happy Christmas

OBJECTIVES
- To learn the Christmas song.
- To learn and consolidate Christmas vocabulary.

LANGUAGE
Happy Christmas. Christmas card, Father Christmas, presents, snowman, star, stocking.

REVISION
Members of the family.

MATERIALS
Banana and Chocolate *flashcards*. A Christmas card. Stickers for this lesson. Photocopies of the Christmas card template (*Resource Bank*, page 89). Crayons. Scissors. Sheets of paper.

Beginning the lesson

- Use the Banana and Chocolate *flashcards*. Have Banana say: *Happy Christmas, Chocolate!*, and Chocolate say: *Happy Christmas, Banana!* Banana and Chocolate then say *Happy Christmas* to the children. Encourage the children to respond. Tell the children they are going to learn about Christmas in this lesson, but first ask them what kinds of things they do at Christmas and what they like about this time of year.

Developing the lesson

- Say: *Open your books at page 70.* Give the children a moment to look at the page and then ask them who they can see (Banana and his family, they are at home at Christmas). Point to the different characters and ask: *Who's this?* Elicit: *Mother, father, brother, sister, baby* and *Banana.* Tell the children that they are going to listen to and learn a Christmas song. Play the recording and have the children point to the different members of the family on the page.

R•44 🎧

Let's be happy	With my father and my mother,
This Christmas,	My sisters and my brothers.
Sing songs and have fun!	Let's be happy
Let's be happy	This Christmas,
This Christmas,	And love everyone.
And love everyone.	

- Repeat the song and encourage the children to sing along.
- Show the children the Christmas card, saying: *Look children! A Christmas card.* The children repeat. Explain that Banana has sent some Christmas cards to his family and show the children the Christmas card stickers for this lesson. Go over or teach the Christmas vocabulary for the stickers (*star, Father Christmas, snowman* and *presents*). Then show the children how to stick the stickers in

their corresponding places on the page. Say: *The star Christmas card is for Banana's mother and father. The presents Christmas card is for Banana's sister. The snowman Christmas card is for Banana's brother and the Father Christmas card is for the baby.*

Ending the lesson

- Hold up your book and point to the Christmas stockings around the fireplace. Say: *Look! Christmas stockings! Count!* The children count the stockings (there are six). Ask the children who they think the stockings are for (Banana and the members of his family). Hand out the photocopies of the Christmas card template, the scissors and the crayons. First the children colour the Christmas dog. Then show the children how to make the Christmas card by cutting out the dog and sticking it on the front with a slip of paper, The children can complete the message inside and take the cards home to give to their families.

Reinforcement activity

- 🎧 Sing the Christmas song again with the children (R – 44).

Extension activity

- Play *Snowballs*. Hand out sheets of paper, and show the children how to crunch them up to make paper 'snowballs'. Have individual children come and draw the Christmas items on the board, the star, snowman, Father Christmas, presents and the stocking (make sure they are sufficiently big). The children now take turns at trying to hit one of the objects on the board with their 'snowball'. They should first name the object they are going to try and hit. You may wish to play this as a team game.

Happy Easter

OBJECTIVES
- To learn vocabulary related to Easter.
- To learn the Easter song.

LANGUAGE
Happy Easter, Easter rabbit, bunny, chocolate eggs.

RECEPTIVE LANGUAGE
Who's this? Yes, it's the Easter rabbit. Stick the (orange) sticker here. Easter bunnies, (run)!

REVISION
Farm animals. Colours.

MATERIALS
Banana and Chocolate *flashcards*. Crayons. The colour *flashcards*. Chocolate eggs (optional). Prepared egg templates made from card. Pieces of material and ribbons if available. Scissors.

Beginning the lesson

- Use the Banana and Chocolate *flashcards* to greet the children and then have Chocolate turn to Banana and say: *Happy Easter, Banana!* Banana replies to Chocolate: *Happy Easter, Chocolate!* Then have them both turn to the children to say: *Happy Easter!* Encourage the children to reply: *Happy Easter!* Explain to the children that in this lesson they are going to learn about the Easter celebration.

- Play a game with the children. Name an animal (use the animals from unit 6). The children imitate the animal, making the corresponding noise. Finish with *rabbit*. Ask the children what kind of noise they think a rabbit makes.

Developing the lesson

- Say: *Open your books at page 71.* Give the children a moment to look at the page and then ask: *Who's this?* As the children reply *rabbit*, say: *Yes, it's the Easter rabbit.* Ask the children if they know what the Easter rabbit does (he brings and hides the chocolate eggs). Ask them to find the hidden eggs on page 71 (they are under the ground, in the rabbit's 'house'). Hand out the crayons and let the children colour the rabbit in their books in the colours of their choice. As the children work, go round and ask the children to name the colours they are using.

- Now put the set of colour *flashcards* on the board and elicit the colours from the children. Tell the children that they are going to learn a song about the colours of the *flashcards*. Teach *bunny*, explaining that it is another way of saying *rabbit*. Play the song. First let the children listen, then play the song again and encourage the children to identify the colours on the board that are mentioned (orange, purple, yellow, red, blue). Remove the colour *flashcards* not mentioned in the song. Play the song a third time for the children to sing along.

R·45

Come Easter Bunny,
Easter Bunny come!
I like chocolate eggs,
Yum! Yum! Yum!

Orange eggs,
Purple eggs,
Yellow, red and blue.
Chocolate eggs for me,
And chocolate eggs for you!

Come Easter Bunny,
Easter Bunny come!
I like chocolate eggs,
Yum! Yum! Yum!

Ending the lesson

- Show the children the Easter egg stickers for this lesson. Have the children stick them on the eggs in their books. Say: *Stick the (orange) sticker here*, pointing to the space in your book. Continue with the other egg stickers.

- Finally tell the children that they are Easter bunnies. Say: *Easter bunnies, run! Easter bunnies, jump!*

Reinforcement activity

- If available, hide chocolate eggs in the classroom and have a 'chocolate egg hunt'.

Extension activity

- Make decorated eggs. Hand out the egg templates made from card and have the children decorate them with different colours, or with different materials, ribbons, etc. The children can then take them home to give to their families for Easter.

TEACHING NOTES

Resource bank

FUN ENGLISH

My English dictionary

1. **Drawings in the air:** The children have their books open at the picture dictionary page. Choose an item from the page and draw the outline in the air. The children try to guess what you have drawn.

2. **Miming words:** The children work in groups. They take turns to choose a word from the page and then mime it for their group to guess the word.

3. **Drawings on backs:** The children work in pairs. They take turns to choose a word from the page and then draw it on their partner's back with their finger, the partner tries to guess the word.

4. **Whispering words:** Choose a word and whisper or mouth it for the class to guess.

5. **Chinese whispers:** Get the class into teams and have each team stand in a line. Choose one of the words from the dictionary page and whisper the word to the first child in each line. On the word *Go!* the children whisper the word down the line. The first child at the end of the line to shout out the word correctly, wins a point for their team. Change the order of the children in the lines and continue the game.

6. **Bingo (1):** Use the picture dictionary page to play *Bingo!* The children will need small pieces of paper. As the words are called out they should cover them on the page with the pieces of paper. When the children are confident with the game, have them cover up two or three words (of their choice) before playing. With stronger classes give complete sentences which include the vocabulary item.

7. **Bingo (2):** The children make their own Bingo grid of (nine) squares, (depending on the language and the class level), and choose the vocabulary items from the picture dictionary page to draw in the squares before playing.

8. **Word associations:** Give the children a few minutes to look at the picture dictionary page, then have them close their books. Call out a word from the page, the children try to say another word from the same word group.

9. **Memory game (1):** Ask the children to look carefully at the picture dictionary page. Give them a limited amount of time to remember the words. The children then close their books and try to recall as many words as they can from the page. With stronger classes you can ask the children about details in the pictures, such as colours and numbers of objects.

10. **Memory game (2):** Start by saying: *In my bag there's a (pencil).* The next child continues: *In my bag there's a (pencil) and a (book).* The children take turns to add new words, but must remember all the items which have gone before. The activity can be adapted to fit the different word groups on the different pages, for example page 42: *I'm wearing a jumper. I'm wearing a jumper and a T-shirt, etc.*

11. **Find something (blue):** Get the class into groups. Ask the children to look at the page and then say: *Find something (blue)!* The first team to shout out a correct answer wins a point.

12. **What is it? (1):** The children work in groups. A child in the group closes his or her eyes and points to something on the page. He or she then tries to guess the word, asking: *Is it (a) ...?,* to try to find the word. The rest of the group answers *Yes* or *No.*

13. **What is it? (2):** In this activity the children play in groups. One member of the group turns around while the others choose something on the picture dictionary page. The child then tries to find the word by asking: *Is it (a) ...?*

14. **Rhyming words:** Have the children try to find words which rhyme on the page. You may wish to use more than one dictionary page for this activity.

15. **Sentence formations:** Have the children look at two of the dictionary pages and then work in pairs to try to make a sentence including a word from each page.

16. **Odd one out:** Prepare a quiz on the board or on sheets of paper for the children. Draw two or three objects from the same word group, plus one item from a different group. The children try to identify the object which doesn't belong. With stronger classes you can have them prepare their own quizzes for each other.

17. **Descriptions:** Provide descriptions or definitions of the pictures, for example, for page 26: *It's big, it's green.* (The Christmas tree). The children try to guess which object or person you are talking about.

18. **Who am I?** Pretend you are one of the objects, animals or people on the dictionary page and describe yourself.

19. **True or false?** Make statements about the things on the page. The children decide if they are true or false. If the statement is true the children stand up, if it is false they remain seated. Invite the children to correct the false statements.

20. **Favourite words:** At the end of each unit have the children choose three or four of their favourite words to learn from the picture dictionary page. Invite the children to make their own personalised records with drawings.

ACTIVITIES

Card games

1. **What's behind my back?** Take one of the cards from the set and put it behind your back. The children try to guess what it is. Continue with the different cards. Repeat using different prepositions and places (the chair, desk, bag, etc.). Use gestures to make your questions clear.

2. **Ordering:** The children have their cards laid out on their desks in front of them. They listen to your instructions and put the cards in the corresponding order.

3. **What's missing?** You will need a tray and a scarf for this game. Lay out a set of the cards on the tray and go through the vocabulary with the children. Then cover the cards with the scarf, remove one without the children seeing, show the children the remaining cards and ask: *What's missing?* When the children are familiar with the game they can play in pairs. One of the children turns round while the other removes one of his or her cards. The child turns back and tries to identify the missing object.

4. **Story sequences:** Prepare a short story which involves the different objects or things from the cards in a particular sequence. The children listen and try to sequence the cards according to the order in the story. You can use adaptations of the stories in *Fun English 1* or stories the children already know to help the children's comprehension.

5. **Banana says:** The children have their cards laid out in front of them. Say: *Banana says, hold up the (apple).* The children hold up the corresponding card. If you don't include *Banana says,* the children don't respond.

6. **Parrots:** Show one of the cards to the children and say: *It's a (fridge).* If the statement is true, the children should repeat it. If the statement is false they should remain silent. You can play this as a team game and ask individual children in the teams to respond. Give points for a correct response.

7. **What is it?** Place the set of cards in an envelope and slowly start to reveal one of them. The children try to guess what it is without seeing the whole image. (Alternatively you can have the card appear from behind a book).

8. **Memory game:** The children play in groups with two sets of the cards. Have them place the cards face down on a desk, mixed up. The children take turns to turn over two cards to try to find a matching pair. As they turn the cards over they name the objects they reveal. If the cards are the same the children keep the pair and continue.

9. **Snap:** Play this game in groups. The children place their cards upside down in front of them, in a pile. They take turns to reveal a card and say what it is. If the card is the same as the object that went before, the children shout *Snap!* The first child to shout *Snap!* keeps the pair, but must be able to name the object. The child with the most pairs at the end wins.

10. **Numbers game:** The children work in groups and 'pool' their cards. Practise the vocabulary with numbers by saying: *Show me (three) pigs.* The children look through their cards to find and hold up three 'pig' cards. The first group to do so wins a point.

11. **Happy families:** The children play in groups of four. They 'pool' their cards and then hand out four to each child. The rest of the cards are placed upside down in the centre of the desk. The children try to collect a group of four cards which are the same. They take turns to ask each other: *(María), have you got a (banana)?* If *(María)* has a *(banana)* she hands the card over and the child continues to ask the other children in the group. If the answer is *No,* the child takes a card from the pile in the centre, but must put down another one next to it.

12. **Odd one out:** Prepare a quiz with the sets of cards for the children. Put together two or three objects from the same card group, plus one item from a different group. The children try to identify and name the object which doesn't belong. With stronger classes you can have them prepare their own quizzes for each other with their cards.

13. **Bingo!** The children use their cards to make a Bingo 'board'. They should select their cards (give the children a specific number) and lay them out in front of them to form the 'board'. Now play *Bingo!* As you call out the objects the children turn their cards over.

14. **Chain game:** Have the children stand in a circle with their cards in their hands. A child starts and names one of the objects on his or her cards, showing it at the same time. The next child continues and shows and names a different object. This continues until you say *Change!,* at which point the direction changes and the 'chain' starts to go in the opposite direction. As the children become familiar with the game, speed it up.

15. **Cops and robbers:** This activity works well at the end of the year for consolidation of the course vocabulary. You need a large space to play this game, preferably outside. Divide the class into two groups, the 'cops' and the 'robbers'. Stand the groups behind lines facing each other. Put different objects on the ground selected from the cutout cards from different units. When you shout out the name of an object, the 'robbers' run and try to pick it up and take it back across their line. If the 'cops' touch them before they cross their line they have to return the object.

green

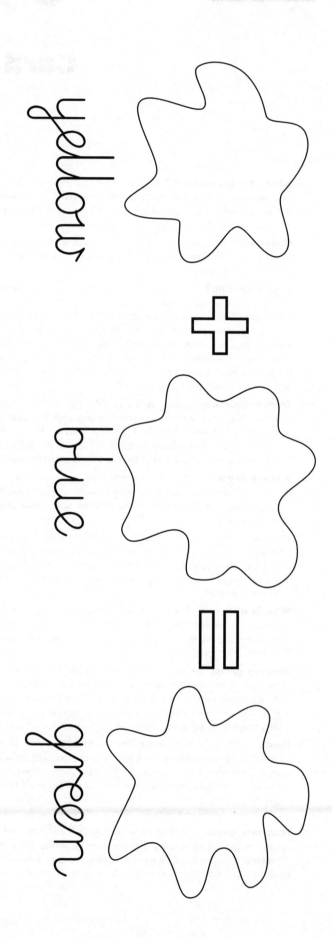

+

red

=

brown

yellow

+

blue

=

green

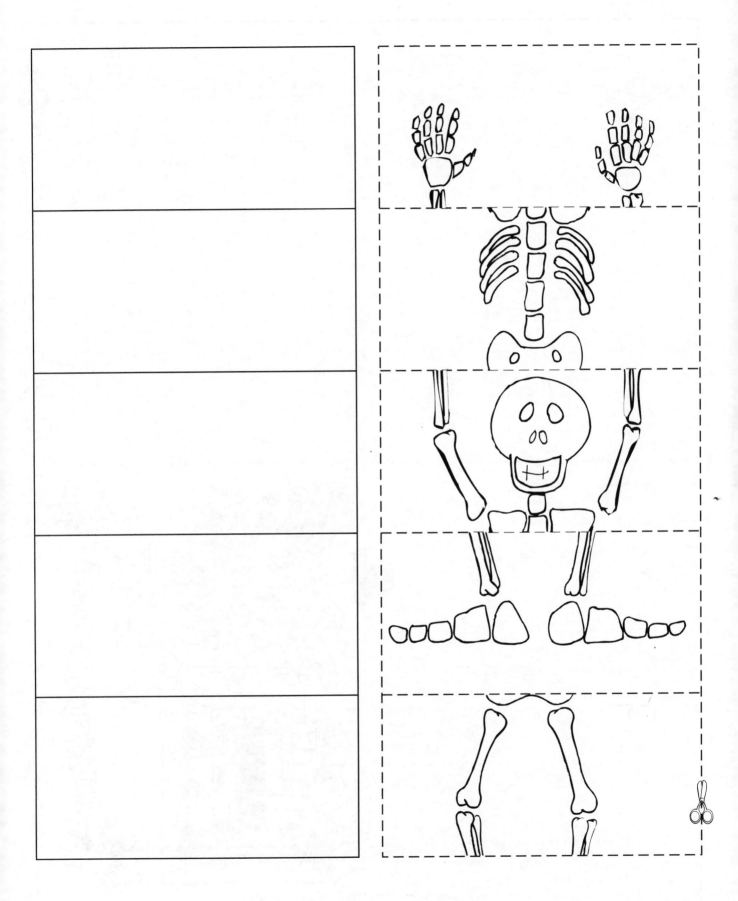

fold

RESOURCE BANK

stick here - stick here - stick here - stick here - stick here - stick here -

fold

81

PHOTOCOPIABLE © PEARSON EDUCATION 2003

fold

fold

fold

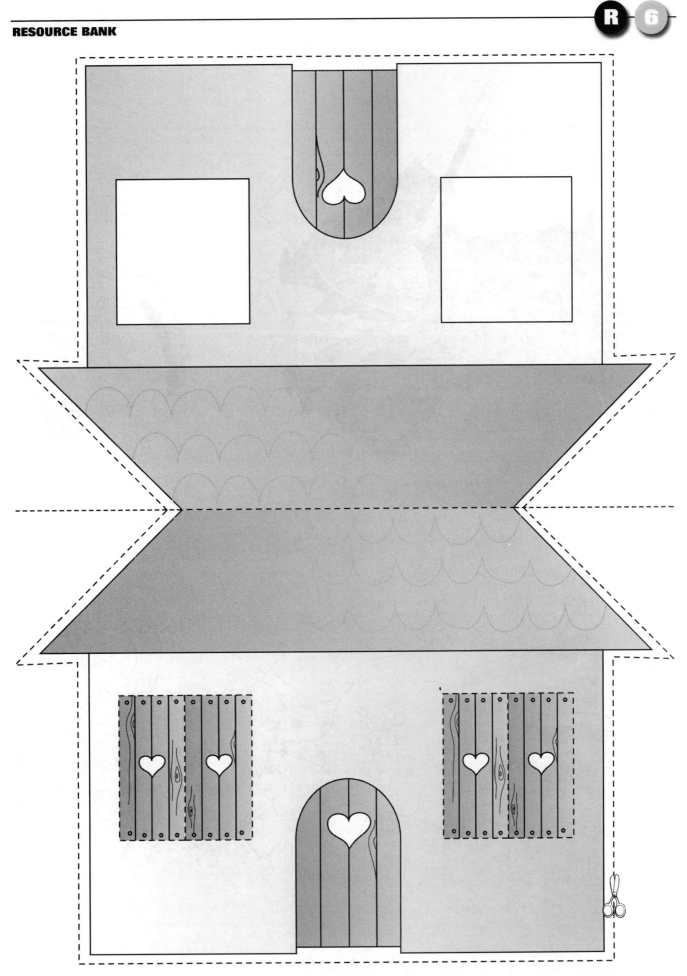

83

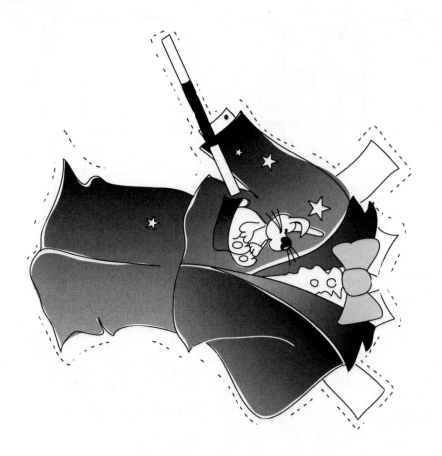

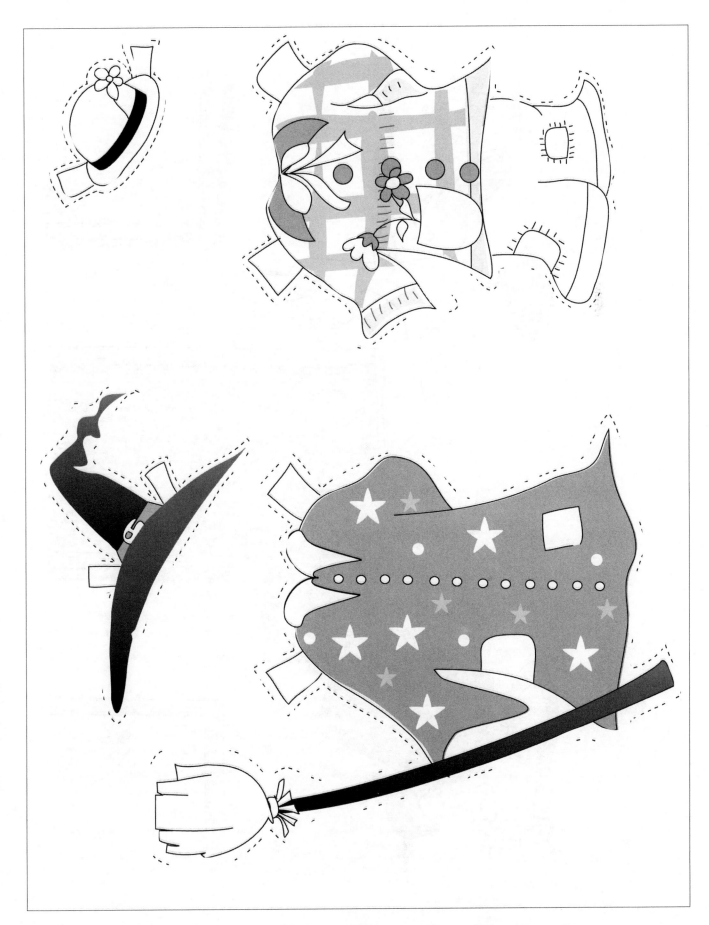

85

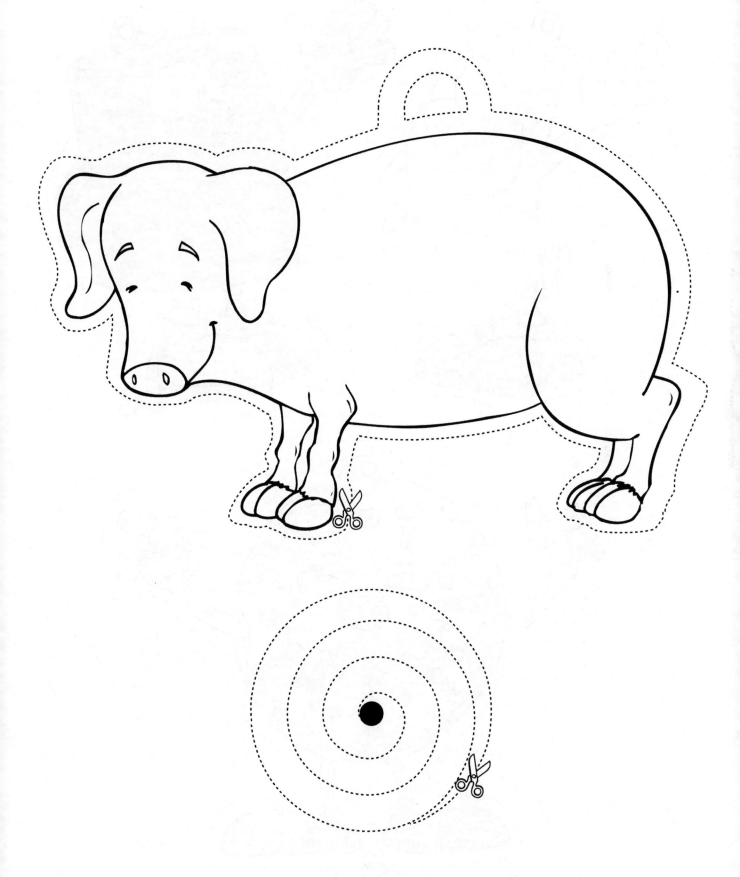

fold

Happy Christmas
Happy Christmas
Happy Christmas
Happy Christmas
Happy Christmas

Evaluation

FUN ENGLISH

EVALUATION

CLASS ACTIVITIES CHART

CLASS: _____

UNIT:		LESSON:	

ACTIVITIES:	

OBJECTIVES:	

PUPIL'S NAME	COMMENTS
1	
2	
3	
4	
5	
6	
7	
8	
9	
10	
11	
12	
13	
14	
15	
16	
17	
18	
19	
20	
21	
22	
23	
24	
25	

EVALUATION

E V A L U A T I O N

REVISION SHEET CHART

PUPIL'S NAME	REVISION SHEET							
	1	2	3	4	5	6	7	8
1								
2								
3								
4								
5								
6								
7								
8								
9								
10								
11								
12								
13								
14								
15								
16								
17								
18								
19								
20								
21								
22								
23								
24								
25								

MARKING CRITERIA: ★=still developing   ★★=progressing well   ★★★=excellent

REVISION SHEET 1:	Max. 8	1-3 ★	4-6 ★★	7-8 ★★★
REVISION SHEET 2:	Max. 9	1-3 ★	4-6 ★★	7-9 ★★★
REVISION SHEET 3:	Max. 10	1-3 ★	4-6 ★★	7-10 ★★★
REVISION SHEET 4:	Max. 8	1-3 ★	4-6 ★★	7-8 ★★★

REVISION SHEET 5:	Max. 10	1-3 ★	4-6 ★★	7-10 ★★★
REVISION SHEET 6:	Max. 10	1-3 ★	4-6 ★★	7-10 ★★★
REVISION SHEET 7:	Max. 10	1-3 ★	4-6 ★★	7-10 ★★★
REVISION SHEET 8:	Max. 11	1-3 ★	4-7 ★★	8-11 ★★★

Revision Sheet 1

Listen and circle

- Tell the children to circle the objects they hear you say. Say each sentence twice.

  Number one. Circle the pencil.
  Number two. Circle the chair.
  Number three. Circle the book.
  Number four. Circle the teacher.

4 marks

Listen and colour

- Ask the children to take out the following crayons: blue, yellow, green and red. Tell the children to colour the numbers, according to your instructions. Say each sentence twice.

  Colour number one blue.
  Colour number two yellow.
  Colour number three green.
  Colour number four red.

4 marks

Marking instructions
Count the number of correct answers and indicate with a tick in the correct box. The children can colour the stars if they wish.

Revision Sheet 2

Listen and circle

- Tell the children to circle the things they hear you say. Say each sentence twice.

  Number one. Circle the big witch.
  Number two. Circle the big monster.
  Number three. Circle the small cat.
  Number four. Circle the small ghost.

4 marks

Listen and colour

- Ask the children to take out the following crayons: brown, orange, blue, green and red. Tell the children to colour the different things and parts of the body, according to your instructions. Say each sentence twice.

  Colour the monster brown.
  Colour the pumpkin orange.
  Colour the witch's eyes blue.
  Colour the witch's nose green.
  Colour the witch's mouth red.

5 marks

Marking instructions
Count the number of correct answers and indicate with a tick in the correct box. The children can colour the stars if they wish.

Revision Sheet

Count and circle

- Tell the children to circle the number of objects that you say for each group. Say each sentence twice.

  Number one. Circle three snowmen.
  Number two. Circle one Father Christmas.
  Number three. Circle four Christmas trees.
  Number four. Circle five stars.
  Number five. Circle six presents.

5 marks

Listen and number

- Tell the children to number the family members by writing the corresponding number next to each picture, according to your instructions. Say each sentence twice.

  Number one. Banana's sister.
  Number two. Banana's father.
  Number three. Banana's mother.
  Number four. The baby.
  Number five. Banana's brother.

5 marks

Marking instructions
Count the number of correct answers and indicate with a tick in the correct box. The children can colour the stars if they wish.

Revision Sheet

Listen and circle

- Tell the children to circle the objects they hear you say. Say each sentence twice.

  Number one. Circle the sofa.
  Number two. Circle the bath.
  Number three. Circle the bed.
  Number four. Circle the fridge.

4 marks

Listen and draw

- Go over the vocabulary in the boxes first with the children (*cat, Banana, Chocolate, witch*). Tell the children to draw the characters in the house, according to your instructions. Say each sentence twice.

  Draw the cat in the bedroom.
  Draw Banana in the kitchen.
  Draw Chocolate in the living room.
  Draw the witch in the bathroom.

4 marks

Marking instructions
Count the number of correct answers and indicate with a tick in the correct box. The children can colour the stars if they wish.

Revision Sheet

Count and circle

- Tell the children to circle the number of objects that you say for each group. Say each sentence twice.

  Number one. Circle two jumpers.
  Number two. Circle five hats.
  Number three. Circle four dresses.
  Number four. Circle one T-shirt.
  Number five. Circle six shoes.
  Number six. Circle three shirts.

6 marks

Listen and colour

- Ask the children to take out the following crayons: green, brown, blue and yellow. Tell the children to colour Banana and Chocolate's clothes, according to your instructions. Say each sentence twice.

  Colour Banana's hat green.
  Colour Banana yellow.
  Colour Chocolate's hat blue.
  Colour Chocolate brown.

4 marks

Revision Sheet

Listen and circle

- Tell the children to circle the animals they hear. Say each sentence twice.

  Number one. Circle the dog.
  Number two. Circle the sheep.
  Number three. Circle the pig.
  Number four. Circle the cow.
  Number five. Circle the horse.
  Number six. Circle the duck.

6 marks

Listen and draw

- Go over the vocabulary in the box first with the children (*rabbit, chick*). Tell the children to draw the animals on the farm, according to your instructions. Say each sentence twice.

  Draw seven chicks on the farm.
  Draw eight rabbits on the farm.

4 marks

Marking instructions
Count the number of correct answers and indicate with a tick in the correct box. The children can colour the stars if they wish.

Marking instructions
Count the number of correct answers and indicate with a tick in the correct box. The children can colour the stars if they wish.

Revision Sheet 7

Count and circle

- Tell the children to count and circle the corresponding number of fruits, according to your instructions. Say each sentence twice.

  Number one. Circle five lemons.
  Number two. Circle nine pears.
  Number three. Circle seven strawberries.
  Number four. Circle eight apples.
  Number five. Circle six oranges.
  Number six. Circle ten bananas.

6 marks

Listen and match

- Ask the children to listen and draw a line to match the characters with the corresponding fruits, according to your instructions. Say each sentence twice.

  Banana's father's got a lemon.
  Banana's mother's got a strawberry.
  Banana's brother's got a pear.
  Banana's sister's got an apple.

4 marks

Revision Sheet 8

Listen and number

- Tell the children to number the toys by writing the corresponding number next to each picture, according to your instructions. Say each sentence twice.

  Number one, the ball.
  Number two, the teddy bear.
  Number three, the bike.
  Number four, the doll.
  Number five, the lorry.
  Number six, the car.

6 marks

Listen and match

- Ask the children to listen and draw a line to match the characters with the corresponding toys, according to your instructions. Say each sentence twice.

  Banana's got a bike.
  Chocolate's got a ball.
  Banana's sister's got a car.
  Banana's brother's got a lorry.
  The baby's got a teddy bear.

5 marks

Marking instructions
Count the number of correct answers and indicate with a tick in the correct box. The children can colour the stars if they wish.

Marking instructions
Count the number of correct answers and indicate with a tick in the correct box. The children can colour the stars if they wish.

Listen and circle.

1.

2.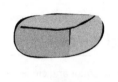

3.

4.

Listen and colour.

    7-8   4-6   1-3

98

Listen and circle.

1.

2.

3.

4.

Listen and colour.

    7-9   **4-6** **1-3**

  **heet**

NAME: _____

CLASS: _____

Count and circle.

1.

2.

3.

4.

5.

Listen and number.

   7-10   **4-6** **1-3**

NAME: _____

CLASS: _____

Listen and circle.

1.

2.

3.

4.

Listen and draw.

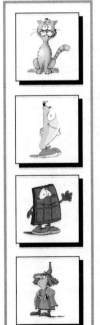

 **7-8**   **4-6** **1-3**

Count and circle.

1.

3.

5.

2.

4.

6.

Listen and colour.

Listen and circle.

1.

4.

2.

5.

3.

6.

Listen and draw.

   7-10   **4-6**   **1-3**

R evision S heet 7

NAME: _____
CLASS: _____

Count and circle.

1.

3.

5.

2.

4.

6.

Listen and match.

  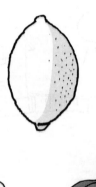    

7-10   4-6   1-3

EVALUATION

Listen and number.

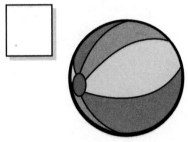

Listen and match.

 **8-11**   **4-7** **1-3**

NOTES

NOTES

NOTES

NOTES